COOK SIMPLE

effortless cooking every day

COOK SIMPLE

DIANA HENRY

photographs by Jonathan Lovekin

MITCHELL BEAZLEY

to Gillies, with love

Cook Simple
by Diana Henry

First published in Great Britain in 2007 by Mitchell
Beazley, an imprint of Octopus Publishing Group Limited,
Carmelite House, 50 Victoria Embankment,
London EC4Y 0DZ
www.octopusbooks.co.uk

An Hachette UK company
www.hachette.co.uk

This paperback edition published in 2010
Reprinted in 2013, 2015, 2016, 2017, 2020

A CIP catalogue record for this book is available from the
British Library.

ISBN 978 1 84533 574 8

Commissioning Editor: Rebecca Spry
Art Director: Tim Foster
Designer: Miranda Harvey
Editors: Susan Fleming, Debbie Robertson
Proofreader: Jamie Ambrose
Home Economist: Sarah Lewis
Production Controller: Lucy Carter
Index: John Noble

Typeset in Garamond and Din
Colour reproduction by Sang Choy, Singapore
Printed and bound in China

contents

· · · · · · ·

introduction

· · · · · ·

A keen cook, I used to dash around convenience stores after work trying to think of something for supper, envying those who could spend more time in their kitchens. I'm not an aficionado of the ready meal. Even after a tough day I prefer to spend 15 minutes cooking spaghetti and tossing it with olive oil, garlic and chilli than the same amount of time waiting to eat the contents of a foil tray that will feed only one person when it says it will do two.

But when I had a baby my cooking changed. 'Quick' cooking was no longer the answer; I couldn't stir a risotto for 25 minutes with a baby on my hip. I needed *effortless* cooking. I had to find simple ways to turn the building blocks of meals – chicken thighs, chops, a few red peppers – into something that would make me salivate as well as sustain me.

The first thing I did was bung nearly everything in the oven, which takes less time than you'd think. A jointed chicken cooks in 40 minutes, a small leg of lamb in 50 and fillets of fish in 12. An ever-growing range of marinades kept me roasting and baking meat and vegetables for months. When I got tired of marinating, I served roasted meat and fish with pestos, salsas and savoury butters that could be whizzed in the blender. I plundered the cuisines of every country I could think of for ways to accessorize simple offerings.

Even puddings got the oven treatment. Baked fruit might sound boring, but try it doused in red wine and cassis, cooked *very* slowly and served with a big bowl of cream – better than any slaved-over bit of *pâtisserie*. One-dish cooking also became vital: vegetables were stuck in with the meat and I acquired winning ways with little potatoes, roasting them with spices, glazed with balsamic vinegar or drizzled with pesto. Green salad became ubiquitous.

There are plenty of faster dishes in this book, too. Lots of them are quite restaurant-y and ideal for last-minute supper parties. Seared tuna or chicken can be dressed up with the same sauces as roast food. A bag of leaves can be tossed with other ingredients – figs, Parma ham and pomegranate seeds, for instance – which require only a bit of shopping.

Finding ways of cooking that involve spending no more than 15 minutes at the kitchen counter (though the dishes might take longer to cook) has made me more creative: I have looked again at what I can do with a jar of tahini, a can of anchovies or a bag of pears. It has also made me more sociable. These days I can have friends for supper mid-week (even with a job and two children) and not end up frazzled.

Whether you have a punishing job, are juggling kids, or are single and just want ideas for no-hassle entertaining, if you like your food simple, this book will help you to make it better.

Diana Henry

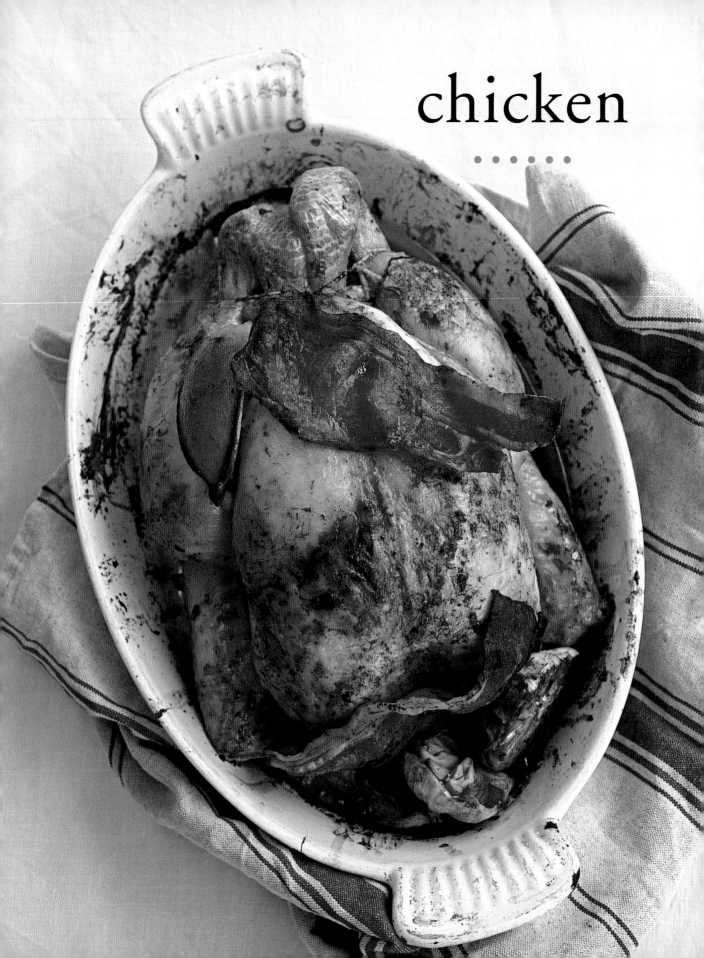

chicken

······

A recipe, from a café in Hawaii, which I have been making for years. There's practically no cooking but everyone loves this dish – it's always hard to resist sweet, honey-glazed meat. Serve with rice and stir-fried greens, or in good weather, a salad of leaves, shredded spring onions and julienned (fine strips) cucumber and carrot.

• • • • • •

pacific lime chicken

serves 4

8 chicken thighs, bone in, skin on

wedges or halves of lime, to serve

marinade

5 tbsp runny honey

5 tbsp dark soy sauce

juice of 4 limes

3 tsp soft brown sugar

3 garlic cloves, crushed or grated

leaves from 5 sprigs thyme

black pepper

I Mix all the marinade ingredients together. Make incisions in the underside of the chicken and pour the marinade over it. Cover with cling film. If you have time, leave the chicken to marinate – anything from 15 minutes to the whole afternoon – in the refrigerator, turning the chicken pieces every so often.

2 Lift the chicken out of the marinade and put it in a small roasting tin or shallow *gratin* dish; it needs to lie in a single layer. Roast in an oven preheated to 190ºC/ 375ºF/gas mark 5 for 35-40 minutes, basting every so often with the leftover marinade and the cooking juices until cooked through. If it gets too dark in colour, cover the dish with foil. The finished dish will be sticky and glossy. Serve with fresh limes, cut into wedges or halves.

and also...

...roast catalan chicken

Cook in the same way as above but make the marinade from 4 tbsp olive oil, 8 tbsp runny honey, the juice of 1 lemon, 1 tbsp ground cumin, 6 crushed garlic cloves, salt and pepper. Serve with little roast potatoes and a big green salad.

Here is good old roast chicken and then some. I like it because all the veggies are served in one dish and there's no gravy to make: just prepare the sauce in advance and spoon the cooking juices over the meat.
In summer, I don't even bother to roast the tomatoes – simply toss in halved cherry tomatoes. And instead of potatoes, you could serve rinsed cannellini beans straight from the can.

. . . . . .

roast chicken with warm vegetables and rocket cream

serves 4-6

olive oil

1 x 1.8kg (4lb) roasting chicken

salt and pepper

300g (10½oz) cherry tomatoes on the vine

600g (1lb 5oz) small waxy potatoes

200g (7oz) green beans, topped, but leave the tails intact

juice of ½ small lemon

rocket cream

125g (4½oz) mayonnaise

100g (3½oz) fromage frais

75g (2¾oz) rocket

I Drizzle olive oil over the chicken and season it. Roast in an oven preheated to 200°C/400°F/gas mark 6 for 1½ hours. The chicken is cooked when the juices that run from between the leg and breast are clear, without any pink.

2 Meanwhile, put the tomatoes in a roasting tin, season and drizzle with a little olive oil, then roast in the same oven as the chicken for 25 minutes.

3 Whiz all the ingredients for the rocket cream in a food processor. Scrape into a bowl and store in the refrigerator.

4 With 20 minutes' roasting time left, boil the potatoes in salted water for about 15 minutes until tender, then drain. Cook the beans in boiling water for about 5 minutes to retain some crunch. Drain and rinse in cold water so that they stay green.

5 Slice the potatoes. Put these, the beans and the roast tomatoes into a bowl and gently toss them with salt, pepper, 3 tbsp extra-virgin olive oil and the lemon juice.

6 Divide the vegetables among plates and carve the chicken, or serve the chicken on a big warm platter with the vegetables spooned around it. Serve the rocket cream in a bowl or sauce boat on the side.

There are different kinds of *chorizo* sausage – some you have to cook, others you can either cook or eat as they are, and a few you don't cook at all. Try to get the second type for this dish. *Chorizo* also comes in sweet and hot forms, so use whichever you prefer.

· · · · · ·

chicken and chorizo in rioja

serves 4

1 tbsp olive oil

salt and pepper

8 chicken thighs

1 celery stalk, finely chopped

1 large onion, halved and cut into slim slices

2 red peppers, halved, deseeded and cut into strips

300g (10½oz) *chorizo* sausage (papery skin removed), cut into 5mm (¼in) thick rounds

1½ tbsp plain flour

200ml (7fl oz) red Rioja or other red wine

200ml (7fl oz) chicken stock

3 sprigs thyme

1 bay leaf

2 tbsp chopped flat-leaf parsley, to serve

I Heat the oil in a broad shallow casserole in which the chicken can lie in a single layer (I use a shallow 30cm/12in Le Creuset pan). Season the chicken and quickly colour it on both sides. You just want to colour the outside, not to cook it through. Remove the chicken and set aside.

2 Add the celery, onion, peppers and *chorizo* to the pan in which you have cooked the chicken and, over a medium heat, cook until the vegetables have softened, stirring frequently, about 10 minutes. Add the flour and stir it in over a low heat for about 1½ minutes, then pour on the wine. Let this bubble away for a few minutes, then add the stock. Bring to the boil, then turn down to a simmer and put the chicken back into the pan, skin-side up. Season, going easy on the salt as both the wine and the *chorizo* add their own saltiness. Tuck in the thyme and bay leaf. Cook in an oven preheated to 180°C/350°F/gas mark 4 for 35 minutes until the chicken is cooked through. Leave the lid off the whole time – this will help the liquid reduce and further brown the chicken skin – but do baste the top of the chicken with the juices every so often.

3 Sprinkle with flat-leaf parsley and serve in the casserole in which it was cooked.

serves 4

salt and pepper

4 large chicken breasts, skin removed

olive oil

1 large onion, finely chopped

450g (1lb) Greek yogurt

2 large eggs, beaten

2 tbsp plain flour

55g (2oz) feta cheese, crumbled

2 tbsp chopped dill

leaves from 2-3 mint sprigs, torn

3 garlic cloves, crushed

40g (1½oz) Parmesan, freshly grated

I Season the chicken breasts and quickly brown them in a couple of tbsp of olive oil – you just want a good outside colour, not to cook the chicken through. Remove these and set aside. Sauté the onion in the same pan – add a little more oil if you need to – until soft and just turning golden.

2 Combine everything else, except the Parmesan, in a large bowl and mix well.

3 Lay the onion and the chicken in the bottom of an ovenproof dish into which everything will fit snugly. Spread the yogurt mixture evenly on top and sprinkle with the Parmesan.

4 Cook in an oven preheated to 180ºC/350ºF/gas mark 4 for 45 minutes. The yogurt will have set and the chicken should be cooked through.

A smart idea from the Greeks and a lovely supper dish. The chicken cooks in a golden blanket of yogurt and cheese, set to a soft custard.

· · · · · ·

greek baked chicken in yogurt

This simple recipe revolutionized my cooking. There's no browning and everything's cooked together in one dish, just bunged in the oven. It's based on one in Antonio Carluccio's book, *An Invitation to Italian Cooking*, and is what home cooking should be: chunky, rustic and deeply savoury.

· · · · · ·

chicken baked with red onions, potatoes and rosemary

serves 4

2 red onions, each cut into 10 wedges

550g (1¼lb) waxy baby potatoes, not peeled

2 garlic bulbs, separated into cloves, but not peeled

salt and pepper

8 tbsp extra-virgin olive oil

2 tbsp balsamic vinegar

about 5 sprigs rosemary

1 x 1.8kg (4lb) chicken, jointed into 8 pieces, or 8 chicken thighs, rubbed with sea salt to crisp the skin

I Spread the vegetables and garlic in a single layer over the base of a huge roasting tin so that they will crisp and brown beautifully. Season, pour over the oil and balsamic vinegar and add the rosemary, leaving some sprigs whole and stripping the leaves off the rest. Toss the vegetables with your hands and tuck the chicken pieces in among them. Bake for 45 minutes at 200°C/400°F/gas mark 6 until cooked through.

2 Transfer everything to a big platter – or take to the table in the roasting tin. Serve a green salad on the side.

and also...

...with sweet potato, smoked paprika, olives and pickled lemons

A popular and more exotic take on the above. Marinate 8 chicken thighs in 4 tbsp olive oil, 1 tbsp smoked paprika, 5 crushed garlic cloves and the finely sliced flesh of ½ preserved lemon plus 2 tbsp juice from the jar of lemons. Put into a roasting tin as above, with 900g (2lb) unpeeled sweet potatoes, cut into big chunks; 2 red onions, cut into wedges; and seasoning. Bake for 45 minutes, until cooked through in an oven preheated to 200°C/400°F/gas mark 6, adding a handful of stoned black olives and the shredded rind of the lemon 15 minutes before the end. Scatter with chopped parsley and mint or coriander and serve.

We start on the stove-top with this recipe for a change. As long as you find thin-skinned oranges, you actually can eat the wedges.

. . . . . .

turkish chicken with oranges and warm spices

serves 4

15g (½oz) unsalted butter

1 tbsp olive oil

8 chicken thighs, seasoned with salt and pepper

2 red onions, halved and cut into wedges

2 thin-skinned oranges, unpeeled, each cut into 8 wedges

5 garlic cloves, crushed

1 small red chilli, halved, deseeded and finely chopped

3 tsp ground coriander

1 cinnamon stick

75g (2¾oz) raisins, soaked in boiled water for 30 minutes and drained

juice of 1 orange

150ml (5fl oz) chicken stock

1½ tbsp thyme honey

a small handful of mint leaves

I Heat the butter and oil in a shallow casserole and brown the chicken thighs on each side. Lift out the chicken and set aside. Add the onion and orange to the pan and sauté for 2-3 minutes. Add the garlic, chilli, dried spices and raisins and cook for another 2-3 minutes. Pour on the orange juice, stock and honey. Season and simmer for 10 minutes.

2 Put the chicken back in the pan, cover and cook over a low heat for 20-25 minutes, or until the chicken is cooked through. Check the seasoning, scatter the mint over the top and serve with Greek yogurt and rice.

and also...

...spanish chicken with sherry and pine nuts
Brown chicken thighs as above, then add 100g (3½oz) soaked raisins and 350ml (12fl oz) medium sherry. Cover and simmer on a low heat for 20-25 minutes, until cooked. Scatter with 35g (1¼oz) toasted pine nuts and chopped parsley. Serve with olive-oil-roasted potatoes.

There's nothing like charred meat, herbs and the crunch of sea salt to get the juices flowing. Thighs have a much better flavour and texture for grilling than chicken breasts.

· · · · · ·

griddled chicken with thyme and sea salt

serves 4

8 boned chicken thighs with skin on, opened out flat

4 tbsp olive oil

chopped leaves from about 10 sprigs thyme

salt and pepper

juice of 1 lemon

lemon wedges, to serve

I With a very sharp knife, make some slits in the chicken thighs on both sides. Rub them with the olive oil and pat on the thyme leaves. Cover and leave to marinate in the refrigerator overnight, or for a couple of hours.

2 Heat a griddle pan until it is really hot. Season the oiled and herbed chicken and put it onto the griddle pan, skin-side down. Let it sizzle and splatter for 2 minutes. Turn the chicken over and let it cook for another 2 minutes. Lower the heat and continue to cook until the thighs are done all the way through – about another 5 minutes – turning once more.

3 Squeeze over the juice of a lemon and serve immediately with lemon wedges.

and also...

...with coriander and chilli butter

Marinate the chicken in olive oil as above (omit the thyme), then mix 75g (2¾oz) softened butter with the shredded flesh of 2 medium red chillies (halved and deseeded), a handful of fresh coriander leaves, 1 fat crushed garlic clove and a good squeeze of lime. Put the butter in the refrigerator to get really cold. Griddle the chicken as above and serve with a pat of butter melting over the top and some wedges of lime.

...with black olive and anchovy butter

Again, marinate the chicken in olive oil as in the first recipe (omit the thyme), then mash together 75g (2¾oz) softened butter with 3 chopped anchovy fillets, 1 crushed garlic clove, pepper, a good squeeze of lemon juice and 25g (1oz) chopped pitted black olives. Refrigerate. Griddle the chicken as above and serve knobs of the butter melting over it.

chicken

Spanish rice dishes, such as this, are a real boon for the tired cook. Unlike risottos, you can just leave them to look after themselves – you must *not* stir them. It used to be difficult to find paella rice, but now many supermarkets stock it.

· · · · · ·

arroz con pollo y chorizo

serves 6

8 tbsp olive oil

salt and pepper

12 chicken thighs, bone in and skin on

2 red peppers, deseeded and sliced

250g (9oz) *chorizo*, cut into small chunks

1 large onion, roughly chopped

4 garlic cloves, crushed

3 tsp smoked paprika

1 tsp dried chilli flakes

1.3 litres (2¼ pints) chicken stock

375g (13oz) Spanish Calasparra rice (paella rice)

2 tbsp chopped flat-leaf parsley

juice of 1 lemon

extra-virgin olive oil

and also...

...caribbean lazy chicken and rice

This was given to me by food writer Richard Cawley. As long as you don't overdo the hot sauce, children love it. Marinate 8 chicken thighs with 4 crushed garlic cloves, the juice of a lime, leaves from 4 sprigs thyme and ½ tbsp West Indian hot sauce (or other chilli sauce). Wash 175g (6oz) basmati rice until the water runs clear, then put the rice, 1 chopped onion and 175g (6oz) sliced mushrooms into a shallow ovenproof dish. Lay the marinated chicken on top in a single layer and pour on the marinade. Season well and pour on 575ml (a scant pint) hot chicken stock. Cook, uncovered, for 45 minutes in an oven preheated to 200°C/400°F/gas mark 6 until cooked through. A spinach and avocado salad is good alongside.

I Heat the olive oil in a broad shallow pan, season the chicken thighs and brown on all sides. Take the chicken out of the pan and set aside. Add the peppers and *chorizo* to the same pan and sauté over a medium heat until the peppers are softening. Throw in the onion and garlic and cook until the onion is soft. Stir in the paprika and chilli and cook for a minute, then add the chicken stock. Put the chicken pieces back and simmer, covered, over a gentle heat for 15 minutes.

2 Most people don't have a pan big enough to fit all the chicken in a single layer and still have room for the rice, so transfer the chicken, vegetables and stock to a big, wide ovenproof dish – the one I use for this is 33cm (13in) in diameter. Pour the rice round the chicken and season really well. Put in the oven, preheated to 180°C/350°F/gas mark 4, and cook for 20 minutes, until the stock has been absorbed and the top is golden. When cooked, cover the dish with foil and leave for 5 minutes. Scatter with parsley and lemon juice and drizzle with olive oil to serve.

Small effort, big taste and big impact. Serve on a bed of couscous (see the recipe on page 189; the more jewelled the better) and sing *Marrakesh Express* (or *Midnight at the Oasis* or similar) as you carry it to the table.

· · · · · ·

serves 4

8 tsp coriander seeds

8 tsp cumin seeds

8 tsp harissa

8 tbsp olive oil

salt and pepper

4 poussins

coriander and mint leaves, olive oil and lemon to serve

north african spiced poussins

I Dry-fry the coriander and cumin seeds in a small frying pan for a couple of minutes, just to release their fragrance. Grind them in a mortar and pestle and add the harissa and olive oil, salt and pepper.

2 Season the inside of the birds and paint the spice paste onto the skin. Roast in an oven preheated to 200°C/400°F/gas mark 6 for 45-50 minutes, or until the poussins are cooked through.

and also...

...poussins with *gremolata*, pasta and peas

Rub 4 poussins all over with about 55g/2oz softened butter and season. Roast for 45-50 minutes in an oven preheated to 200°C/400°F/gas mark 6 and check for doneness. Mix the zest of 1 unwaxed lemon with 2 finely chopped garlic cloves and good handful of finely chopped flat-leaf parsley. Scatter this *gremolata* over the poussins and serve with small pasta shapes which you've mixed with cooked peas, seasoning and a good slug of extra-virgin olive oil.

...poussins with lemon, orange and oregano

Mix together the zest of 1 orange and 1 lemon, the juice of 4 oranges and 1 lemon, 6 tbsp balsamic vinegar, 125ml (4fl oz) olive oil, 6 crushed garlic cloves and 3 tbsp dried oregano. Marinate the poussins in this, covered, for a couple of hours or overnight in the refrigerator, turning them every so often. Season and put in a roasting tin with 3 oranges and 2 lemons cut into wedges (drizzle the fruit with a little olive oil and season) and roast as above. Spoon the marinade over the birds every so often during the roasting. When cooked, remove the poussins and boil the cooking juices to thicken them. Serve the poussins with the reduced juices and charred wedges of fruit.

It's a pity we think of stuffings mainly as accompaniments to the Christmas turkey. They're a great way to turn plain roasts into something special, and the most inexperienced of cooks can make them. These recipes give you enough to stuff a 1.8kg (4lb) chicken or boned leg of lamb, or 4 poussins.

· · · · · ·

lots of ideas for stuffings

All of these should be stuffed into the cavity of a bird or inside a boned leg of lamb before cooking. If you prefer not to stuff poultry, bake the stuffing alongside the meat, covered with foil for 30 minutes, then remove the foil and cook for another 10 minutes.

chorizo, red pepper and potato
Sauté 150g (5½oz) sliced *chorizo* (pull the papery skin off first) with a chopped and deseeded red pepper and 2 tbsp olive oil. Add 200g (7oz) finely cubed waxy potatoes (don't worry about peeling them) and cook for another couple of minutes, until the potato is pale gold and the pepper is quite soft. Season and add some chopped parsley or fresh coriander and a squeeze of lemon. Let the stuffing cool. Good for chicken or poussins.

potato, olive, fennel and pancetta
Remove any tough outer leaves from 2 fennel bulbs. Trim at the top and base, quarter the bulbs and remove the core. Discard these bits but keep any little fronds of fennel to add to the final stuffing. Chop the fennel flesh then sauté it in 3 tbsp olive oil with 200g (7oz) finely cubed waxy potatoes (no need to peel them), ½ finely chopped small onion, 55g (2oz) chopped black olive flesh and 100g (3½oz) finely cubed pancetta. Add the grated rind of ½ lemon, season and leave to cool. Use to stuff chicken, poussins or boned leg of lamb.

watercress, apricot and hazelnut
An idea shamelessly stolen – and little changed – from the wonderful chef, Shaun Hill. Sauté a finely chopped onion in 25g (1oz) butter. Mix with 75g (2¾oz) finely chopped dried apricots (the kind that don't need soaking), 100g (3½oz) wholemeal breadcrumbs, 55g (2oz) halved, toasted hazelnuts and 55g (2oz) chopped watercress leaves. Season, then add 25g (1oz) butter, cut into little chunks, and 1 beaten egg. Combine everything well. Use to stuff chicken or poussins.

georgian stuffing
Gorgeous and exotic. You can use dried sour cherries – soaked and drained – in place of the pomegranate seeds. Just mix 75g (2¾oz) walnut pieces with 200g (7oz) crumbled feta cheese, 3 crushed garlic cloves, the seeds from ½ ripe pomegranate, a handful of chopped fresh coriander, 4 tbsp olive oil and seasoning. Stuff a chicken or poussins with this, drizzle with olive oil, and scatter on salt, pepper and ½ tbsp ground cayenne. Roast and serve with wedges of lemon, a green salad and a big bowl of bulgar wheat.

fruited couscous
Pour 125ml (4fl oz) boiling water or stock over 125g (4½oz) couscous and leave for 15 minutes. Fork

through the grains to separate them, add 2 tbsp of olive oil and season well. Stir in 100g (3½oz) chopped dried fruit (soaked and drained – raisins, apricots, cherries and cranberries are all good) and the zest and juice of ½ lemon. The shredded rind of ½ preserved lemon is good, too, and you can add chopped pistachios or almonds as well, plus chopped parsley, mint or coriander. For chicken, poussins or a boned leg of lamb.

prune, sausage and brandy

Put 150g (5½oz) pitted and chopped prunes in a small saucepan and pour over enough brandy just to cover. Simmer over a very low heat for 15 minutes. The fruit will plump up. Sauté a finely chopped onion in 35g (1¼oz) butter until soft, then add 250g (9oz) sausage meat and cook until pale gold. Add 1 tart chopped apple (cored but not peeled), the zest and juice of ½ orange, 45g (1½oz) breadcrumbs, a good handful of chopped parsley or some thyme leaves and season. Mix and add the prunes and their soaking liquid. Leave to cool. For chicken or poussins.

aliza's chestnut, cranberry and oat

Don't just use this at Christmas or Thanksgiving (it's my friend's Thanksgiving stuffing) – it's too good. Sauté 1 roughly chopped small onion in 75g (2¾oz) butter until soft but not coloured. (You can also sauté finely cubed pancetta or bacon, or chunks of sausage meat with the onion.) Add 75g (2¾oz) fresh cranberries and cook until they have softened, then add 75g (2¾oz) dried cranberries and 4 heaped tbsp cranberry sauce or jelly. Stir until the jelly or sauce has melted, then add 150g (5½oz) oatmeal, 150g (5½oz) cooked vacuum-packed chestnuts (roughly chopped) and season really well. Stir. The mixture should be quite moist and shiny – add more butter if it isn't. Leave to cool. Use to stuff chicken or poussins.

aubergine and date

One for using to stuff boned lamb. You could serve the tahini dressing on page 118 on the side, or a bowl of yogurt seasoned with some chopped mint and crushed garlic. Cut an aubergine into small cubes and sauté in a frying pan in 3 tbsp olive oil until golden on all sides. Season and put into a bowl. Using another 2 tbsp olive oil, sauté ½ finely chopped onion until soft but not coloured. Add a crushed garlic clove and 1 tsp ground cinnamon and cook for another minute. Stir into the aubergine along with 200g (7oz) chopped stoned dates, the juice of ½ lemon, salt and pepper and 12 torn mint leaves.

cherry and dill

Scandinavian-inspired and lovely with chicken in the spring. Sauté a finely chopped medium onion in 55g (2oz) butter until soft but not coloured. Mix this into 150g (5½oz) white breadcrumbs, 85g (3oz) chopped watercress (leaves and fine stems only) and 115g (4oz) dried pitted sour cherries that have been soaked in boiling water for 15 minutes and drained. Add a beaten egg, a small bunch of chopped dill leaves, salt and pepper. Eat your stuffed chicken with a bowl of sour cream mixed with chopped cucumber and a crushed clove of garlic.

polish stuffing

Melt 45g (1½oz) butter in a frying pan and cook a small, finely chopped onion until soft but not coloured. Add 100g (3½oz) finely chopped chicken livers and cook for a few more minutes. Put into a bowl with 100g (3½oz) good cooked ham, chopped (get stuff cut from a whole ham at the butcher's or deli counter), 300g (10½oz) white breadcrumbs, 4 tbsp chopped dill, 1 small beaten egg and seasoning. Mix everything together. Use to stuff a chicken and serve with roast beetroot (see page 126), drizzled with a little buttermilk or daubed with soured cream.

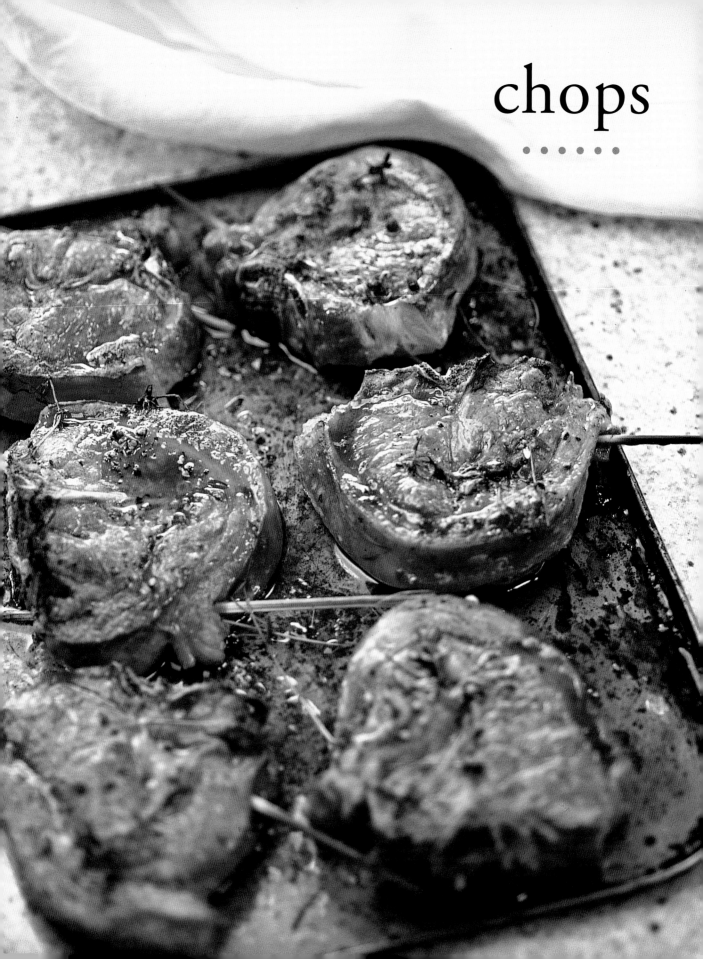

chops

This is good for a sunny spring or summer evening. I'm a big fan of frozen peas: they're sweet, a fantastic colour and, since they are frozen so soon after picking, often taste better than ones you buy and pod yourself. You can use basil or coriander leaves instead of mint; the results are just very different.

· · · · · ·

lamb chops with pea and mint purée

and also...

...with ligurian broad bean purée
Cook 450g (1lb) podded broad beans (fresh or frozen) in boiling water until tender. Drain and, if you have the time, slip the skins off the beans; if you don't, just leave them on and you'll have a rougher purée. Put the beans in a food processor with 2 garlic cloves, 12 mint leaves, 5 anchovy fillets and 4 tbsp freshly grated pecorino cheese. Using the pulse button, make a rough purée while adding 10 tbsp extra-virgin olive oil. Add the juice of ½ lemon, taste, season and blend again. Cook the lamb chops as above and serve with the purée, which can be warm or at room temperature. This purée is also good with grilled chicken or just on rounds of grilled ciabatta.

serves 4

8-12 lamb cutlets (the number depends on size and hunger)

olive oil

salt and pepper

fresh mint and/or wedges of lemon, to serve

pea purée

250g (9oz) fresh or frozen peas

55g (2oz) butter

1 tbsp double cream

salt and pepper

about 8 mint leaves

a squeeze of lemon juice

I Cook the peas in boiling water until tender, then drain. Add the butter and let it melt, then tip the peas into a blender or food processor. Add the cream, seasoning, mint and lemon juice and blend until smooth. You can make the purée in advance and heat it again at the last minute.

2 Heat a ridged griddle pan or a frying pan for the chops. If you're going to griddle them, brush them with olive oil and season; if you're going to use a frying pan, heat a film of oil in it and season the chops. Cook the chops on a high heat until browned on both sides but still pink in the middle. I cook cutlets for about 4 minutes in all, but I do like them rare. You can cut into the flesh of one side to see whether they're done the way you like them.

3 Serve with the warm pea purée, wedges of lemon (good squeezed over the chops – has an effect like salt) and sprigs of mint.

Pomegranate molasses is a sweet-sour (though more sour than sweet) Middle Eastern syrup made from pomegranate juice. It's particularly good with lamb and makes a great sticky glaze. Fresh pomegranate seeds are guaranteed to make any simple dish exotic.

· · · · · · ·

pomegranate and honey glazed chops with radish and cucumber tzatziki

serves 4

8 chunky lamb chops, about 150g (5½oz) each

olive oil

salt and pepper

marinade

2½ tbsp pomegranate molasses

10 tbsp olive oil

1½ tbsp runny honey

2 garlic cloves, crushed

2 tsp cayenne pepper

radish and cucumber tzatziki

100g radishes, very finely sliced

½ cucumber, cut into small cubes

350g (12oz) Greek yogurt

2 garlic cloves, crushed

2 tbsp mint leaves, roughly chopped

2 tbsp olive oil

to serve

a small bunch of mint leaves or coriander (about 30g/1¼oz)

extra-virgin olive oil

lemon juice

seeds from ½ ripe pomegranate (see page 104)

1 Mix the marinade ingredients together. Put the chops into this and make sure they get well coated. Cover with cling film and refrigerate for anything from 1-24 hours.

2 To make the tzatziki, simply mix the radish, cucumber, yogurt and garlic together. Stir in the mint leaves and olive oil.

3 Heat a thin film of oil in a frying pan and cook the chops for about 3 minutes on each side. You want to get a good colour on the outside but must avoid burning the honey and pomegranate mixture, so cook over a moderate heat.

4 Serve the chops on a bed of fresh mint or coriander dressed lightly with extra-virgin olive oil and a squeeze of lemon juice, with the tzatziki on the side. Scatter pomegranate seeds over the top of the tzatziki just before serving – any sooner and the seeds bleed into the yogurt – or over the chops and coriander if you prefer.

serves 4

50ml (2fl oz) olive oil

finely grated zest and juice of 1 lemon

2 garlic cloves, crushed

1 tsp each of ground sweet paprika, cinnamon, cayenne pepper, cumin, coriander and allspice

salt and pepper

8 chunky lamb chops, about 150g (5½oz) each

salad

1 large onion, finely chopped

5 tbsp olive oil

125g (4½oz) Greek yogurt

40g (1½oz) walnut pieces

juice of 1 lime

2 garlic cloves, finely sliced

a small handful of mint leaves, chopped

75g (2¾oz) fresh dates, stoned and finely sliced

This salad is based on an Iranian recipe in Arto der Haroutunian's inspiring book, *Middle Eastern Cookery*. Eat with warm flatbread or a bowl of couscous, rice or bulgar wheat. A little dish of shredded preserved lemon rind is lovely with the sweetness of the lamb and dates and the acidity of the yogurt.

• • • • • •

spiced lamb with date, walnut and yogurt salad

1 Mix the olive oil with the lemon juice and zest, garlic and all the spices and seasonings. Put the lamb chops in this and cover with cling film. Marinate in the refrigerator for anything from two to 24 hours, turning the chops over every so often.

2 For the salad, fry the onion gently in 2 tbsp of the olive oil until really soft and a little golden. Stir in the yogurt, two-thirds of the walnuts, and the lime juice. Spread this in a broad shallow bowl. Heat the rest of the olive oil and quickly fry the garlic until just golden. Add the mint and cook for another 20 seconds or so. Drizzle this on top of the yogurt and onion mixture, then scatter on the dates and the remaining walnuts.

3 You can either fry the chops or cook them on a ridged griddle pan. If you're using a frying pan, you need to heat a couple of tbsp of olive oil in the pan. If you're griddling them, just heat the griddle until it's really hot and put the chops onto it. Cook the chops on a high heat until browned on both sides, then turn the heat down and cook further – about 3 minutes per side in all – but keep them pink and tender in the middle. Serve with the salad.

and also...

...with salsa *mishmish*

A Middle Eastern sauce, probably Iranian in origin. Sauté a finely chopped onion in 2 tbsp olive oil until soft and golden, then add ½ tsp ground cinnamon and a 5cm (2in) chunk of peeled fresh root ginger, finely chopped, and cook for another minute or two. Add 250g (9oz) 'no need to soak' dried apricots and 250ml (9fl oz) chicken stock. Simmer for about 30 minutes, or until the mixture is thick. You can either leave the texture like this or purée it. Add the juice of a lemon; I sometimes add a bit of hot chilli sauce as well. Stir in a good handful of chopped fresh mint or coriander leaves and serve with the lamb. This sauce is also great with grilled or roast chicken.

Harissa is a very hot Moroccan chilli paste, which is quite easy to find in large supermarkets these days. You can blend the chickpeas roughly so that you are left with more of a mash than a purée if you want something to get your teeth into.

• • • • • •

harissa-marinated lamb with chickpea purée

serves 4

2½ tbsp *harissa*

3 garlic cloves, crushed

8 tbsp olive oil

juice of ½ lemon

a good handful of mint leaves, torn

8 chunky lamb chops, preferably from the chump end, about 150g (5½oz) each

salt

chickpea purée

1 x 400g can chickpeas, drained

175ml (6fl oz) olive oil, plus extra if frying the onions

juice of 1 lemon

1 garlic clove, crushed

½ tsp cayenne pepper

1 tsp ground cumin

salt and pepper

2 tbsp chopped coriander leaves

1 onion, roughly chopped (optional)

I Mix the *harissa* with the garlic, oil, lemon and mint and put the chops into it, turning them over to make sure they get well coated. Cover and put them in the refrigerator. Leave them to marinate for anything from 1½ hours to overnight, turning them every so often.

2 To make the chickpea purée, simply chuck everything (except the coriander and the optional onion) into the food processor, with salt and pepper to taste, and blend. The mixture doesn't have to be absolutely smooth. If you can be bothered, fry the chopped onions in a little olive oil until golden brown and slightly singed in some parts. Scatter the onions and the coriander over the purée.

3 Heat a griddle pan for the chops. Salt them at the last minute and then cook them on a high heat for about 3 minutes on each side, until browned but still pink in the middle. You can pierce the flesh to see whether they're done the way you like them.

4 Serve with the chickpea purée. Couscous or bulgar wheat, mixed with plenty of mint or flat-leaf parsley, is a good accompaniment, or just serve with sheets of warm flatbread and maybe a bowl of plain yogurt.

serves 4

1 tart eating apple

300g (10½oz) potatoes, washed (no need to peel them)

1 onion, finely sliced

salt and pepper

55g (2oz) unsalted butter

4 x 250g (9oz) thick pork chops, bone in and partly trimmed of fat

300ml (10fl oz) dry white wine or cider

mustard and thyme butter

55g (2oz) unsalted butter, softened

¾ tbsp grain mustard

leaves from 4 sprigs thyme

A really warming, homely autumn or winter bake. You can use either waxy or floury potatoes in this – each will give a different result. Slices of floury potato will disintegrate, but waxy ones will remain intact. If you can't be bothered to make the butter, just serve the dish as it is with a jar of mustard on the side, and put sprigs of thyme in to bake with the chops.

· · · · · ·

smothered pork chops with mustard and thyme butter

I Halve and core the apple and cut it into wedges about 2.5cm (1in) thick at the thickest part. Slice the potatoes into rounds about the thickness of a pound coin. Toss the potatoes with half the apple and half the onion, and season. Put in the bottom of an ovenproof dish (which will take the chops in a single layer). Dot with half the butter.

2 Melt the rest of the butter in a frying pan. Season the pork chops and quickly brown them on both sides (you just want to colour the meat, not cook it through). Put the chops on top of the vegetables and apple and put the rest of the apple and onion on top. Deglaze the frying pan with the wine or cider by pouring the alcohol into the pan and letting it bubble while you scrape the juices that have stuck to the pan. Pour this over the chops and put in an oven preheated to 180°C/350°F/gas mark 4. Bake for 45 minutes, turning the onions and apples on the top over occasionally so that they get a good all-over colour, until cooked through.

3 To make the mustard and thyme butter, just mash the ingredients together, form into a sausage shape, wrap in cling film or greaseproof paper and chill. Serve a couple of slices of butter on top of each helping.

This Lyon speciality is usually made with chicken joints, but I find that the onions and crunchy breadcrumbs are a winning combination with pork, too. Serve with a green salad and little potatoes roasted in olive oil with garlic.

. . . . . .

pork chops lyonnaise

serves 4

4 x 200g (7oz) pork chops, bone in and partly trimmed of fat

salt and pepper

40g (1½oz) unsalted butter

2 medium onions, finely chopped

1½ tbsp Dijon mustard

leaves from 6 sprigs thyme

45g (1½oz) fresh breadcrumbs

I Season the chops on both sides. Melt 15g (½oz) of the butter in a frying pan and quickly brown the chops, taking care not to burn the butter. Transfer the chops to a shallow ovenproof dish.

2 Sauté the onions in the rest of the butter on a very low heat for about 15 minutes, until they're really soft but not coloured. Stir in the mustard and thyme.

3 Spread the onion mixture thickly over each chop and press the breadcrumbs down on top of that. Bake in an oven preheated to 190ºC/375ºF/gas mark 5 for 35 minutes, or until cooked through, and serve.

Old-fashioned, calorific and just what you need on a winter's night. Mature Cheddar will do if that's all you have, though it doesn't have the same elasticity as melted Gruyère. If you don't have Marsala, try a dryish sherry.

. . . . . .

pork with cheese and marsala

serves 2

6 tbsp olive oil

salt and pepper

2 x 200g (7oz) pork chops, boneless and trimmed of fat

15g (½oz) butter

1 medium onion, finely chopped

2 slices Parma ham

75g (2¾oz) Gruyère cheese, grated

10 tbsp dry Marsala

½ tbsp finely chopped flat-leaf parsley

I Heat the oil in a frying pan. Season the chops and cook for 5 minutes on each side. Take them out of the pan, add the butter to the pan and sauté the onion.

2 Lay a slice of ham on each chop and top with the Gruyère. Cook under a very hot grill for 2-3 minutes, until the cheese bubbles and the chops are cooked through. Meanwhile, stir the Marsala into the onion and bubble away to form enough slightly syrupy sauce to pour around both chops. Scatter with parsley and serve.

I love this dish for its utter plainness. There is something very satisfying about eating a soy-infused bit of pork with nothing more fancy than the zap of lime and fish sauce. You don't really 'dip' the pork in the sauce, but rather spoon it over.

. . . . . .

thai-spiced pork chops with lime dipping sauce

serves 4

6 tbsp sweet soy sauce or kecap manis

salt and pepper

a handful of coriander stalks, finely chopped (keep the leaves for serving)

4 large pork chops (about 200g/7oz each), boneless and partially trimmed of fat

lime dipping sauce

8 tbsp fish sauce

juice of 2 limes

3 shallots, finely sliced lengthwise

1 red chilli, halved, deseeded and finely sliced

coriander leaves from above, about 2 tbsp, coarsely chopped

1 Mix the soy sauce, salt, pepper and coriander stalks in a shallow bowl and add the pork chops. Turn the chops over to make sure they get well coated. Cover loosely with cling film and put in the refrigerator to marinate, preferably overnight. If you can, turn the chops over in the marinade every so often.

2 To make the lime dipping sauce, just mix everything together. Put in a small bowl to serve at the table.

3 Heat a ridged griddle pan and cook the chops over a high heat for 2 minutes on each side to get a good colour, then turn the heat down to medium and cook for about 5 minutes on each side. Check to see that the chops are cooked by piercing the underside (the side you will put on your plate) with a sharp knife and having a look. The meat should be tender but not pink.

4 Serve with the coriander leaves, the lime dressing and some plain boiled rice.

Go to a good butcher and buy thickly cut chops that are organic, or at least outdoor-reared. If he sells pork from breeds such as Gloucestershire Old Spot, even better.

Despite its simplicity, this dish looks so lovely – glossy with honey, crimson juices running out of the plums – that it's special enough to serve to friends mid-week. So much better than 'dinner-party' food.

• • • • • •

pork chops with plums and chinese spices

serves 4

450g (1lb) plums, preferably crimson-fleshed ones

4 x 200g (7oz) pork chops, bone in and partly trimmed of fat

5 tbsp runny honey

1 tsp Chinese five-spice powder

1 tsp ground ginger

1 medium red chilli, deseeded and finely chopped

4 garlic cloves, crushed

juice of ½ orange

1 tsp white-wine vinegar

salt and pepper

I Halve and stone the plums. If they are quite large, cut them into quarters or sixths; small ones need only be halved. Lay the chops in a shallow ovenproof dish and tuck the plums in around them where they can lie in a single layer without overlapping.

2 Mix all the other ingredients together and pour over the chops and plums, turning everything around to make sure all sides are well coated. Bake in an oven preheated to 190ºC/375ºF/gas mark 5 for 45 minutes until cooked through. Serve with rice and stir-fried greens or a watercress or spinach salad.

If you want to do a bit more with this dish, add some rinsed green olives to the pan about 10 minutes before the end of the cooking time.

. . . . . .

spanish pork chops with orange

serves 4

3 tbsp olive oil

salt and pepper

4 pork chops, about 200g/7oz each, trimmed of fat

2 onions, finely chopped

100ml (3½fl oz) sherry vinegar

juice and finely grated zest of 1 orange

300ml (10fl oz) medium sherry

leaves from about 8 sprigs thyme

I Heat the olive oil in a large frying pan and season the chops. Cook them over a high heat for about 2 minutes on each side until golden brown. Take the chops out of the pan and reserve.

2 Cook the onions for 10 minutes in the fat left in the pan, until golden. Add the sherry vinegar, orange juice and rind and sherry. Season, add most of the thyme and bring to the boil. Put the chops back into the pan, cover and turn the heat down low. Simmer for 15 minutes, then remove the lid, turn the chops over and cook, uncovered, for another 15 minutes, until cooked through. Scatter with thyme and serve.

Another of those brilliant Italian dishes that is packed with flavour but requires very little preparation. Serve with green leaves: rocket or watercress.

. . . . . .

italian pork chops with fennel seeds

serves 4

4 x 250g (9oz) pork chops

1 tbsp fennel seeds

1 tsp chilli flakes

¾ tbsp dried oregano

½ tbsp sea-salt flakes

4 garlic cloves, peeled

4 tbsp olive oil

I Make deep incisions along the fat of the chops to help stop them curling as they cook. Crush together the spices, oregano, salt and garlic with the oil in a mortar or a small food processor. Rub this all over the chops. Cover loosely and refrigerate for an hour or so.

2 Heat a frying pan until it is really hot. Put in the chops and cook them for 2 minutes on each side. Transfer them to an ovenproof dish and cook in an oven preheated to 220°C/425°F/gas mark 7 for 20 minutes. Check that the chops are cooked through by piercing them – they should be tender but not pink. Serve with the cooking juices.

If you're always wondering what you can do to jazz up a plain pork chop or roast chicken thighs, here are some answers. Sauces, salsas and relishes that are easy to whip up – and behave well after you've made them – are great, tasty ways to dress up food.

· · · · · ·

sauces, salsas and relishes for chops and other things

mint, almond and honey sauce
Sicilian-inspired, though not authentic. In a blender, put 60g (2¼oz) toasted almonds, 4 garlic cloves, 85g (3oz) mint leaves, 40g (1½oz) flat-leaf parsley (leaves only), 3 tsp runny honey, the juice of 1 lemon, salt and pepper. Purée while adding 300ml (10fl oz) extra-virgin olive oil in a steady stream. Taste in case you want to adjust anything. Brilliant with lamb.

argentinian *chimichuri*
Argentinians eat this with steak. It's also good with roast or grilled lamb or chicken. Into a blender, put a really generous bunch of flat-leaf parsley (leaves only), 3 garlic cloves, 3 tbsp red-wine vinegar, the juice of ½ lime, 2 tbsp oregano leaves, 1 tsp each of ground cumin and smoked paprika, and some salt and pepper. Whiz with 175ml (6fl oz) extra-virgin olive oil (a sturdy one – perhaps Greek would be good

here). You can add a chopped red chilli, too (halved and deseeded first) if you want more bite. Use this soon after you've made it: it's better fresh.

thai cucumber relish
Peel a cucumber and cut in half lengthwise. Scoop out the seeds with a teaspoon and throw them away. Cut the cucumber into fine, half-moon shaped slices. In a bowl, mix 4 tbsp rice vinegar, 3 tsp caster sugar, a good pinch of salt and 2 tbsp hot water. Add 1 medium red chilli, halved, deseeded and chopped, 1 very finely sliced shallot and the cucumber. Mix everything really well and leave to stand for an hour before serving. Good with grilled chicken and pork, and spicy fish cakes.

vietnamese peanut sauce (*nuoc leo*)
Heat 1 tbsp groundnut oil in a frying pan and gently fry 2 chopped garlic cloves and 1 chopped medium red chilli (halved and deseeded). When they begin to colour, add 100g (3½oz) chopped, roasted, unsalted peanuts and stir-fry for a minute without colouring. Add 125ml (4fl oz) chicken stock, 4 tbsp coconut milk, 1 tbsp soft brown sugar, 1 tbsp hoisin sauce and 1 tbsp *nuoc nam* (fish sauce). Simmer until the sauce thickens and oil appears on the surface. Great with roast or grilled skewered chicken.

vietnamese ginger sauce (*nuoc mam gung*)
In a bowl, mix 1 tbsp *nuoc nam* (fish sauce) and 1 tsp honey with the juice of 1 lime. Whisk in 100ml (3½fl oz) groundnut oil, 75g (2¾oz) grated fresh root ginger (previously peeled) and 2 red chillies (halved, deseeded and finely chopped). Use as a dipping sauce for fish, pork, chicken or duck.

vietnamese chilli dipping sauce (*nuoc cham*)
In a mortar and pestle, or a small food processor, pound 4 garlic cloves, 2 red chillies (halved, deseeded and finely chopped), 3 tsp caster sugar, the

juice of 1 lime and 4 tbsp fish sauce. Now add 4-5 tbsp water (according to how strong you want it) and mix well. Good with tuna, pork, duck and chicken.

mango and chilli salsa

Cut the flesh of 1 small, peeled, ripe mango into small cubes then mix with the juice of 2 limes, 3 chopped spring onions, a handful of chopped fresh coriander and 1 red chilli, halved, deseeded and cut into fine shreds. Leave for 30 minutes while the flavours meld, but no longer or the fruit gets too soft. Serve with roast or grilled pork, chicken or lamb, or even seared tuna, especially if you've spiced the meat before cooking.

pineapple and mint salsa

Sister to the one above; use it in the same way. Cut 450g (1lb) pineapple flesh into slices, then quarter each slice and remove the hard bit that goes right through the centre of the pineapple. Cut the flesh into small chunks. Halve 1 medium chilli, deseed and cut the flesh into slivers. Add to the pineapple along with 2 chopped spring onions, 3 tbsp chopped mint leaves, the juice of 1 lime, 2 tbsp olive oil and 1½ tsp caster sugar. Mix together.

pico de gallo

Mexican. Halve and seed 400g (14oz) well-flavoured tomatoes, cut into 5mm (¼in) squares and mix with 2 tbsp finely diced red onion, 1 medium red chilli, halved, deseeded and finely chopped, 2 tsp caster sugar, 2 tbsp finely chopped fresh coriander, juice of 1 lime, 25ml (1fl oz) lager (Mexican if possible!), salt and pepper. Cover and chill for 30 minutes before using. Serve with chicken, pork or steak, with sour cream and sliced avocados alongside.

creamy mustard sauce

An old-fashioned French sauce. Melt 15g (½oz) butter in a small pan and gently sauté 4 chopped shallots until soft but not coloured. Add 50ml (2fl oz) white wine vinegar, turn up the heat and boil to reduce to about ½ tbsp. Add 150ml (5fl oz) dry white wine and reduce by half, then add 200ml (7fl oz) double cream, 1½ tbsp Dijon mustard and a squeeze of lemon. Season and heat through. You want a sauce the consistency of whipping cream, so if it's too thick add a little water. Good with chicken, fish or pork.

saffron cream sauce

Put 150ml (5fl oz) dry white wine in a saucepan and heat until the wine has almost evaporated. Add 350ml (12fl oz) really well-flavoured chicken stock and ½ tsp saffron threads. Boil until reduced by two-thirds, then add 150ml (5fl oz) double cream. Simmer again to reduce the sauce until it is thick enough to coat the back of a spoon. Delicious with poached white fish or sautéed chicken breast.

sauce *vierge*

Warm 100ml (3½fl oz) extra-virgin olive oil (preferably a fruity one from Provence) with 1 garlic clove, bashed with skin on, over a low heat. Remove from the heat and add 6 torn basil leaves and a good pinch of salt. Let the flavours infuse for about 10 minutes, then remove the flavourings. Add the finely chopped flesh of 3 peeled plum tomatoes. You can either gently reheat the oil or serve at room temperature. Add 6 torn basil leaves, and maybe finely chopped stoned black olives, just before serving. Great spooned over plain grilled or roast fish.

zhug

A very hot relish from Yemen. Serve with roast veg or roast or grilled chicken or lamb. It's especially good with cold Greek yogurt to cut its heat. Halve and deseed 3 medium fresh red chillies and 2 red bird's-eye chillies and put them into a food processor with the seeds of 8 cardamom pods, 1½ tsp caraway seeds, 3 garlic cloves and a large bunch of fresh coriander leaves. Add 100ml (3½fl oz) extra-virgin olive oil with the motor running. Taste and add a really good squeeze of lemon. Add salt to taste as well.

sausages

· · · · · ·

I wish I had a pound for every time I've cooked this dish. All you need to do is remember to buy sausages and broccoli on the way home from work and dinner will be on the table in 20 minutes. Chilli flakes are a great thing to keep in your store cupboard.

· · · · · ·

italian sausages with purple-sprouting broccoli, chilli and penne

serves 4

8 Italian or other spicy sausages

6 tbsp olive oil

1 onion

500g (18oz) purple-sprouting broccoli or tender-stem broccoli

4 garlic cloves, finely sliced

1 tsp dried chilli flakes

250ml (9fl oz) dry white wine or dry vermouth

salt and pepper

200g (7oz) penne

3 tbsp extra-virgin olive oil

freshly grated Parmesan, to serve

I Cut the sausages into lengths about the size of half your index finger. Heat the olive oil in a sauté pan (which has a lid) and brown the sausages all over. Scoop out the sausages and set them aside.

2 Halve the onion lengthwise, then cut each half, from tip to root, in crescent-moon-shaped slices about 1cm (½in) thick at the thickest part. Heat the oil which is still in the pan and cook the onion over a fairly brisk heat until golden, but not brown. Add the broccoli and stir it around, then add the garlic and the chilli and cook for about a minute. Put the sausages back in the pan, add the white wine, season and bring to the boil. Immediately turn the heat down, cover and leave to cook for about 7 minutes, until the broccoli is just tender, the sausages are cooked and the cooking juices have reduced.

3 While the sausages are simmering, cook the penne in plenty of boiling salted water until *al dente*. Drain and immediately stir the pasta into the sausage mixture. Check the seasoning, drizzle on the extra-virgin oil and serve with freshly grated Parmesan.

You may only be cooking sausages, but the bunches of baked grapes make this dish look luxurious. Again, this is a dish that is special enough for a supper party.

Saba is grape must. If you can't find it (Italian delicatessens and some supermarkets stock it these days) use either *vincotto* or balsamic syrup mixed half and half with grape juice.

· · · · · ·

vine-growers' sausages

serves 4

1 onion, sliced

2 celery stalks, finely chopped

olive oil

8 good-quality pork sausages

250g (9oz) seedless black grapes

2 bay leaves

salt and pepper

200ml (7fl oz) red wine

50ml (2fl oz) *saba*

I Put the onion and celery in the bottom of an ovenproof dish that will hold the grapes and sausages in a single layer. Season and stir in 2 tbsp olive oil. Lay the sausages and grapes on top (leave about half the grapes on their stalks – it just looks nice). Using a wooden spoon, crush about a third of the grapes so that their juice comes out. Tuck in the bay leaves. Season and drizzle a little olive oil over the grapes and sausages. Mix the wine with the *saba* and pour it around the sausages.

2 Put into an oven preheated to 190ºC/375ºF/gas mark mark 5, and roast for 50 minutes, until cooked through. You can turn the sausages over halfway through the cooking time so that they get coloured on both sides.

Sweet, sour, spicy and very Italian, I think this robust dish is certainly special enough to serve to friends as a hearty supper.

· · · · · ·

salsiccia agrodolce

serves 4

3 tbsp olive oil

8 spicy sausages, preferably Italian

1 onion, coarsely chopped

55g (2oz) pine nuts

2 tsp dried chilli flakes

55g (2oz) currants

2 tbsp red-wine vinegar

1 tbsp caster sugar

425ml (15fl oz) chicken stock

salt and pepper

1 bay leaf and a couple of sprigs of thyme

1 tbsp coarsely chopped flat-leaf parsley

2 tbsp capers, drained of brine, or washed if in salt

I Heat the olive oil in a sauté pan or flame-proof shallow casserole dish. Fry the sausages to brown them on all sides. Turn down the heat and add the onion. Cook gently until soft, then add the pine nuts and cook until lightly coloured. Then add all the other ingredients, except the capers, and bring to the boil.

2 Put in an oven preheated to 180ºC/350ºF/gas mark 4, and cook, uncovered, for 30 minutes, until the sausages are done. Stir in the capers and serve.

Now it's so easy to find vacuum-packed chestnuts, it seems a pity to eat them only at Christmas. Their sweetness and fudginess lift plain dishes to greatness.

· · · · · ·

baked sausages with chestnuts

serves 4

8 good-quality pork sausages

200g (7oz) cooked vacuum-packed chestnuts

300g (10½oz) field mushrooms, cut into thick slices

1 large onion, cut into half-moon-shaped wedges

1 garlic bulb, cloves separated but not peeled

10 tbsp olive oil

4 sprigs rosemary

1 bay leaf

salt and pepper

300ml (10fl oz) red wine

I Put everything except the red wine into a broad, shallow casserole or ovenproof dish. Turn the ingredients over so that they get coated in olive oil. Put into an oven preheated to 190ºC/375ºF/gas mark 5 and roast for 25 minutes. Pour in the wine and cook for another 25 minutes. The sausages and vegetables will cook and brown, and the wine will reduce, leaving you with a gorgeous dark and bubbling dish.

2 Serve with mash or olive-oil-roasted potatoes, or just some bread and a salad of winter leaves such as chicory, radicchio and spinach.

4 tbsp olive oil

200g (7oz) bacon lardons

12 good-quality sausages, preferably Toulouse

1 onion, chopped

1 celery stalk, chopped

2 carrots, cut into small cubes

1 x 400g (14oz) can tomatoes in thick juice

2 x 410g (14½oz) cans cannellini beans, one drained, the other not

275ml (9½fl oz) wine, stock or water

1 bay leaf, a small handful of parsley leaves and the chopped leaves from 3 sprigs thyme

2 tsp caster sugar

55g (2oz) fresh white breadcrumbs

salt and pepper

I love *cassoulet,* the sausage, duck confit and bean dish beloved of southwest France, but it takes an age to make. This is my lazy person's substitute. It never ceases to amaze me how a dish which looks totally unappetizing raw turns into this thick, dark, unctuous stew.

• • • • • •

simple gascon sausages and beans

I Heat the oil in a frying pan and brown the bacon and sausages all over. Put them into a shallow broad casserole or ovenproof dish. Add everything else, except the breadcrumbs, and season really well. Sprinkle a third of the breadcrumbs on top and cook in an oven preheated to 180°C/350°F/gas mark 4 for 2 hours. Sprinkle on the rest of the breadcrumbs in two separate goes during the cooking time. Stir in the previous sprinkling of crumbs before adding the next lot.

2 Taste the stew and adjust the seasoning towards the end of the cooking time – beans take a lot of flavouring.

and also...

...chilli sausages and beans

Make as above but add 2 red chillies, halved, deseeded and chopped, and 2 tsp ground cumin. If you don't have fresh chillies, use a chilli sauce such as Tabasco instead. You can also use kidney beans or mixed beans. Stir a handful of coriander leaves into the pot before serving with some wedges of lime and a bowl of sour cream on the side.

serves 2

2 sweet potatoes

1 red onion, halved and cut into half-moon-shaped slices

1 green pepper and 1 red pepper, deseeded and sliced into broad strips

olive oil

1½ tsp smoked Spanish paprika

¼ tsp ground cumin

salt and pepper

200g (7oz) *chorizo*, cut into thick rounds

100g (3½oz) bacon (or pancetta), cut into meaty chunks

2 garlic cloves, finely chopped

1 tbsp chopped coriander or parsley leaves

2 large eggs

A meal you can eat with just a fork, this is perfect, comforting mid-week food. Smoked paprika is available in many delis nowadays.

· · · · · ·

spanish sweet potato with chorizo, peppers and fried egg

I Cut the sweet potatoes into chunks – you don't have to peel them – and put in a small roasting tin with the onion and peppers. Add 2 tbsp olive oil, the smoked paprika, cumin, salt and pepper. Stir the vegetables round until they're coated in oil and spices. Roast in an oven preheated to 200°C/400°F/gas mark 6 for about 30 minutes, or until all the vegetables are tender and slightly charred.

2 Heat 1 tbsp olive oil in a frying pan and cook the *chorizo* and bacon until coloured. Turn the heat down, add the garlic and cook for another minute. Add all this to the cooked vegetables. Stir in the chopped herbs.

3 Heat a little more oil in the same frying pan and fry the eggs. Serve the sweet potato mixture topped with the fried eggs.

I really cheat with sausages: I brown them only if I have time or it's crucial to the dish, but more often than not I just stick them straight in the oven.

• • • • • •

baked sausages with leeks, apples and cider

serves 4

3 leeks, washed and chopped into 2.5cm (1in) lengths

2 apples, halved, cored and cut into wedges

8 good-quality pork sausages

4 tbsp olive oil

salt and pepper

25g (1oz) butter, in small pieces

250ml (9fl oz) medium cider

2 tbsp wholegrain mustard

I Put the leeks and apples into an ovenproof dish and arrange the sausages in a single layer on top. Drizzle over the olive oil, season and toss everything around. Dot the top with the knobs of butter and pour in the cider. Bake in the oven preheated to 190ºC/375ºF/gas mark mark 5 for 50 minutes to an hour.

2 About 10 minutes before the end of cooking time, spread the grain mustard over the sausages and any sticking-out apple pieces, and return to the oven.

3 Serve with creamy mash or some little rosemary-roasted potatoes.

These always go down really well, whether they're served in hot dog rolls – perfect for Halloween – or with buttery roast onions and mashed potato.

• • • • • •

honey and mustard glazed sausages

serves 4

2 big tbsp runny honey

1½ tbsp wholegrain mustard

12 good-quality pork sausages

I Mix the honey and mustard in a bowl. Add the sausages and turn them around in it. Put the sausages into a shallow baking dish and roast for about 25 minutes in an oven preheated to 200ºC/400ºF/gas mark 6. Turn the sausages round every so often and baste them with their juices. The sausages will end up glazed and sticky.

and also...

...maple and mustard glazed sausages
Make as above, but substitute maple syrup for honey.

If you can't find *merguez* sausages use other spicy sausages but let them cook on the vegetables for 25 minutes. Regular sausages are much thicker than *merguez* so need longer cooking.

. . . . . .

merguez sausages with roast peppers and cucumber tzatziki

serves 6

4 peppers, a mixture of red and yellow

1 red chilli, halved and deseeded

450g (1lb) plum tomatoes, halved

1 large red onion, halved and cut into crescent-shaped slices

about 5 tbsp olive oil

salt and pepper

6 sprigs thyme

250g (9oz) tomato passata

12-16 *merguez* sausages

about 2 tbsp coarsely chopped flat-leaf parsley

cucumber tzatziki

½ cucumber

2 garlic cloves, crushed

200g (7oz) Greek yogurt

1½ tbsp extra-virgin olive oil

2 tbsp chopped mint leaves

I Cut the peppers in half, and then into broad slices, about 8mm (⅜in) wide at the thickest part. Slice the chilli into fine strips. Put all the vegetables, the chilli, 3 tbsp of the olive oil, the seasoning and the thyme into a wide cast-iron or stainless-steel sauté pan where they can lie pretty much in a single layer. Toss everything around with your hands to make sure there's a good coating of olive oil, and roast in an oven preheated to 180°C/350°F/gas mark 4 for 40 minutes.

2 Make the tzatziki. Grate the cucumber coarsely and then squeeze out the excess water by pressing the flesh in your hands. Add it to the other ingredients, season, mix well, cover and chill until you need it.

3 Heat the remaining oil in a frying pan until really hot and quickly brown the sausages on all sides. Set them aside. When the vegetables have just 15 minutes' cooking time to go, take them out of the oven and stir in the tomato passata. Season and add the sausages – just set them on top – and return to the oven.

4 Serve in the dish in which it has cooked, sprinkled with parsley, accompanied by the tzatziki and warm flatbread or couscous.

leg of
lamb

Lamb and anchovies are a match made in heaven: the saltiness of the anchovies somehow counteracts the sweetness of the lamb and at the same time emphasizes it. The fish melt into the meat, seasoning it as they disintegrate.

You don't have to finish this off with cream – the cooking juices are good served just on their own – but it works, even though mixing anchovies and cream seems like a culinary culture clash.

· · · · · ·

roast leg of lamb with anchovy cream

serves 6

1 x 1.8kg (4lb) leg of lamb
25g (1oz) butter, slightly softened
1 x 40g (1½oz) can anchovies, drained and chopped
4 garlic cloves, peeled and crushed
freshly ground black pepper
leaves from 4 sprigs thyme
600ml (20fl oz) dry vermouth
200ml (7fl oz) water
150ml (5fl oz) double cream

I Trim the lamb of any scraggy bits of fat. Make deep incisions all over the leg. Mash together the butter, anchovies, garlic, pepper and thyme. (You can blend these in a small food processor or with a pestle and mortar, or just a fork and a small bowl.) Push the butter down into the incisions.

2 Put the lamb in a roasting tin and cook at 220°C/425°F/gas mark 7 for 15 minutes, then turn the heat down to 190°C/375°F/gas mark 5 and cook for a further 50 minutes. Add half the vermouth once the lamb has roasted for 20 minutes, and the rest after it has been cooking for 40 minutes.

3 Remove the lamb to a hot platter, cover with foil, insulate it (I use some old tea towels) and leave to rest for 15 minutes.

4 Add the water to the roasting tin and set it over a high heat. Dislodge the cooking juices from the tin using a wooden spoon – you want to get all the flavour in the pan. Boil the cooking juices until they have reduced by a third, then add the cream. Boil again until you have a slightly syrupy sauce. Serve the lamb with the sauce.

serves 6

1 x 1.8kg (4lb) leg of lamb

2 fat garlic cloves, cut into slivers

2 sprigs thyme

55g (2oz) butter, slightly softened

salt and pepper

225ml (8fl oz) dry cider

a good slug of Calvados or brandy

575ml (19fl oz) chicken or lamb stock

200g (7oz) crème fraîche

We so often partner lamb with Mediterranean flavours – tomatoes and olives, for example – that it's good to find a dish from an area famed for its lamb and dairy produce. Serve this with flageolet beans (canned ones, drained, are fine) heated with a generous knob of butter, salt and pepper, a squeeze of lemon and a handful of chopped parsley. Put the lamb on a warm platter, spoon the parsleyed beans around it and you'll be off looking for your Jacques Brel CD.

· · · · · ·

normandy roast lamb with cider

I Trim the lamb of any raggedy bits of fat. Make small incisions all over the leg and stuff each hole with a sliver of garlic and a little bit of thyme. Rub the butter over the joint, stuffing some of it down inside the incisions, then season really well. Roast in an oven preheated to 220ºC/ 425ºF/ gas mark 7 for 15 minutes, then turn the heat down to 190ºC/375ºF/gas mark 5 and cook for another 50 minutes.

2 Put the lamb on a heated platter, cover with foil and cover with tea towels to insulate it so that the joint can rest for 15 minutes.

3 Pour the roasting juices into a jug and skim off the fat. Set the roasting tin over a medium heat and deglaze the pan with the cider and Calvados. Boil until the liquid is reduced by two-thirds, then add the stock and cooking juices. Boil until this is reduced by two-thirds, then add the crème fraîche. Boil until slightly syrupy. Serve the lamb on a heated platter with the sauce in a warm gravy-boat.

This is adapted from a recipe by Franceso Quirico, published in *The Guardian*. It's a fail-safe, no-hassle Sunday-lunch dish. Stick the lamb in the oven and you can read the papers and talk to your friends instead of conducting the military operation that is the 'Sunday roast'.

You might think cheese and lamb would be strange together, but it works. Roast tomatoes and maybe a plain green salad are all you need with it. The joy of this dish is its simplicity, so don't go overboard on the accompaniments.

· · · · · ·

agnello con patate arraganate

serves 6

1.5kg (3lb 5oz) potatoes, cut into chunks all the same size

3 tbsp olive oil, plus more for drizzling over the lamb

2 garlic cloves, chopped

leaves from 1 bunch flat-leaf parsley, coarsely chopped

leaves from a good fistful of oregano

30g (1¼oz) pecorino cheese, freshly grated

1 x 1.8kg (4lb) leg of lamb

salt and pepper

I Toss the potatoes in a roasting tin with all the other ingredients (except the lamb). Trim any scraggy bits of fat off the lamb. Set it on top of the potatoes, season it and drizzle with a little olive oil. Cook in an oven preheated to 200ºC/400ºF/gas mark 6 for 1¼ hours.

2 Leave to rest, covered with foil and insulated with tea towels or something similar, for 15 minutes before serving. Put the lamb on a platter with all the vegetables around it.

I know that a leg of lamb seems like an extravagance mid-week, but you have leftovers for eating with Middle Eastern purées such as hummus, or for serving with spicy roast vegetables over several nights.

This is Sicilian in influence – they love the mixture of sweet and savoury, and the island is also home to Marsala – but it's not an authentic Sicilian dish. It feels very spring-like because of the greenness of the pistachios, so makes a good meal for Easter.

· · · · · ·

roast lamb with pistachios, raisins and marsala

and also...

...lamb with capers and preserved lemon

Sauté 1 chopped shallot and 2 chopped garlic cloves in 2 tbsp olive oil until soft, then add 40g (1½oz) each of white breadcrumbs, rinsed capers, chopped flat-leaf parsley, and the finely sliced skin of 1 preserved lemon. Stir in 2-3 tbsp of olive oil until the mixture binds together, then season. Stuff the lamb and roast as above.

...lamb stuffed with tapenade

In a food processor whiz 350g (12oz) pitted black olives, 2 x 55g cans anchovies in olive oil (drained), 2 tbsp rinsed capers, 2 chopped garlic cloves, a good squeeze of lemon, 2 tbsp extra virgin olive oil, leaves from 2 sprigs thyme, 1 tbsp chopped flat-leaf parsley, 1 tbsp brandy and some ground black pepper. Stuff a boned leg of lamb and roast as above.

serves 6

100g (3½oz) raisins
250ml (9fl oz) Marsala
25g (1oz) butter
½ small onion, finely chopped
1 small garlic clove, finely chopped
55g (2oz) shelled pistachios, roughly chopped
30g (1¼oz) white breadcrumbs
1 tsp chopped rosemary leaves
finely grated zest of 1 orange
salt and pepper
1 x 1.3kg (3lb) boned leg of lamb (boned weight)
olive oil
100ml (3½fl oz) dry white wine

I Put the raisins in a small saucepan, cover with 6 tbsp of the Marsala and bring to the boil. Immediately turn off the heat and leave the raisins to soak. Heat the butter in a frying pan and sauté the onion until just browning. Add the garlic and fry for another minute. For the stuffing, stir the onions and raisins with any juice into the pistachios, breadcrumbs, rosemary and orange rind, then season.

2 Trim any raggedy bits of fat from the lamb. Lay out the joint and season the inside. Spread the stuffing over the meat, then roll up the lamb and tie at intervals with string. Smear a little olive oil over the meat and season.

3 Place the lamb in a roasting tin and cook in an oven preheated to 220ºC/425ºF/gas mark 7 for 15 minutes, then reduce to 190ºC/375ºF/gas mark 5 and cook for a further 45 minutes for pink meat. Cover with foil, insulate with tea towels and rest for 15 minutes before carving.

4 Pour the cooking juices into a glass jug and skim off the fat. Deglaze the roasting tin with the white wine and remaining Marsala, add the skimmed juices and boil until the juices are slightly syrupy. Pour through a sieve into a clean saucepan or hot gravy-boat. Serve with the lamb.

We tend not to think of roast lamb as a quick meal, but a medium-sized leg of lamb takes just over an hour to cook.

Goat cheese is delicious with lamb, so try other stuffings based on it – one with soaked dried figs, walnuts and goat cheese is excellent, for example. Though saltier and less creamy, feta is a good substitute for goat cheese.

· · · · · ·

lamb stuffed with goat cheese, blush tomatoes and basil

serves 4

1 x 1.3kg (3lb) boned leg of lamb (boned weight)

salt and pepper

stuffing

150g (5½oz) soft goat cheese, crumbled

175g (6oz) semi-dried tomatoes (sometimes called 'sun-blush'), drained of oil, roughly chopped

55g (2oz) basil leaves, torn

1 garlic clove, crushed

3 tbsp olive oil

I Mix everything for the stuffing together gently – you need to break up the goat cheese but not turn it into a paste.

2 Open the lamb out like a book. Cut some pockets in the thickest parts of the meat – this just gives you extra places into which to stuff the cheese mixture. Season the flesh of the lamb and spread the stuffing over it, pushing the cheese mixture into any pockets you've created. Roll up the joint, tie with string at intervals and season well.

3 Place in a roasting tin and put into an oven preheated to 200°C/400°F/gas mark 6. Cook for 15 minutes at this temperature, then 50 minutes at 190°C/375°F/gas mark 6. Transfer the lamb to a carving board, cover with foil and insulate with clean tea towels. Leave to rest for 15 minutes before slicing.

Nothing more than slightly fancy roast lamb, but the embellishments make all the difference. Serve with the cooking juices, roasted potatoes and green salad.

． ． ． ． ． ．

roast lamb with prosciutto and garlic

serves 6

1 x 1.8kg (4lb) leg of lamb

about 16 garlic cloves, cut into slivers

16 small sprigs rosemary

6 slices prosciutto, cut into 2.5cm (1in)-wide strips

olive oil

50ml (2fl oz) balsamic vinegar

150ml (5fl oz) dry white wine

I Trim the lamb of any raggedy bits of fat. Make incisions all over the leg. Roll a sliver of garlic and a small sprig of rosemary up in a bit of prosciutto. As you make each little bundle, stuff it into an incision in the lamb. Use up all the prosciutto and then stuff the rest of the incisions with the remaining garlic and rosemary. Push the flavourings well into the meat.

2 Season the joint and rub olive oil all over it. Put in a roasting tin and pour the balsamic vinegar and wine over it. Roast at 220°C/425°F/gas mark 7 for 15 minutes, then 190°C/375°F/gas mark 5 for another 50 minutes, basting every so often. When the lamb is ready let it rest, insulating it well, for 15 minutes.

The delicious cooking juices from this recipe mean you don't need to make gravy. Tie the lamb with kitchen string to hold it in shape while it cooks.

． ． ． ． ． ．

sweet herbed ginger roast lamb

serves 4-6

1 x 1.3 kg (3lb) boned leg of lamb (boned weight)

leaves from 2 sprigs rosemary, chopped

leaves from 4 sprigs thyme

grated zest of ½ lemon and juice of 1

4 garlic cloves, crushed

1 x 2.5cm (1in) root ginger, grated

4 tbsp each runny honey and olive oil

45g (1½oz) butter, softened

I Open the leg of lamb so that it lies like a book. Trim off any raggedy bits of fat. Make small incisions all over the flesh. Blend everything else except the butter in a food processor. Reserve 3 tbsp of this mixture and mix the butter with the rest. Rub the butter mixture over the meat, pushing it down into the slits. Re-form the leg and rub with the olive-oil mixture. Cover loosely with cling film and put in the refrigerator for 2–24 hours. Get it to room temperature before roasting.

2 Cook at 220°C/425°F/gas mark 7 for 15 minutes, then at 180°C/350°F/gas mark 4 for an hour. Leave to rest for 15 minutes covered with foil and tea towels.

Cook this in a dish that you can take to the table. I sometimes sprinkle the rice with crumbled feta before serving. Roast tomatoes are good on the side.

· · · · · ·

greek roast lamb on rice and spinach

serves 6

6 tbsp olive oil

300g (10½oz) spring onions, trimmed and chopped

4 garlic cloves, sliced

1 tbsp sweet paprika

1kg (2¼lb) spinach, tough stalks removed, washed and sliced

225g (8oz) basmati rice

a large bunch of mint, leaves only, torn

salt and pepper

1.8kg (4lb) leg of lamb

425ml (¾ pint) chicken or lamb stock

425ml (¾ pint) dry white wine

juice of ½ lemon

100g (3½oz) feta cheese, crumbled (optional)

I Heat half the olive oil in a large frying pan and cook the spring onions until soft and wilted, about 7 minutes. Add the garlic and paprika and cook for another 2 minutes, then scrape into a bowl. Heat the rest of the oil in the same pan and cook the spinach in batches until it wilts. Add each batch to the spring onions. Put the rice in the pan with the last load of spinach and turn it over in the oil for a couple of minutes so that it becomes glossy. Add this to the bowl along with the mint and season well.

2 Put the lamb in a roasting tin or large shallow casserole and season well. Put into an oven preheated to 230°C/450°F/gas mark 8 and cook for 15 minutes. Take the lamb out and turn the oven down to 180°C/350°F/gas mark 4. Spread the rice and spinach mixture around the lamb in the roasting tin. Bring the stock and wine to the boil and pour it on to the rice. Return to the oven and cook for 50 minutes. Keep an eye out to make sure the rice doesn't get too dry; the stock and wine should be completely absorbed during the cooking, but you don't want that to happen too soon. Add more wine or water if you need to.

3 Remove the dish from the oven, cover with foil, insulate with a couple of towels or tea towels, and leave to rest for 15 minutes.

4 To serve, squeeze some lemon over the lamb and rice and sprinkle the feta over the rice if you're using it.

Here, a classic Moroccan marinade, *chermoula,* is rubbed into a butterflied leg of lamb, which your butcher can bone out for you. Roasted flat, you'll be amazed how quickly the meat cooks. Roast lamb on the table in 40 minutes – fantastic! You don't even have to make the purée: hummus or minty yogurt goes well with the lamb, too.

· · · · · ·

chermoula lamb with hot pepper and carrot purée

serves 4

1 x 1.3kg (3lb) butterflied leg of lamb (boned weight), trimmed of excess fat

chermoula

6 tbsp olive oil

1½ tsp ground cumin

½ tsp ground coriander

½ tsp sweet paprika

1 medium red chilli, deseeded and finely chopped

finely grated zest and juice of 1 lime

2 garlic cloves, crushed

leaves from 1 small bunch coriander, chopped

a small handful of flat-leaf parsley leaves, chopped

salt and pepper

pepper and carrot purée

2 red peppers, halved and deseeded

4 tbsp olive oil

2 tbsp red-wine vinegar

450g (1lb) carrots, scraped and chopped

½ tsp cayenne pepper or paprika

2 tbsp double cream (optional)

I Mix all the *chermoula* ingredients together. Pierce the meat all over on both sides with a sharp knife and put in a roasting tin. Pour on the *chermoula* and rub it all over, making sure it gets into the little cuts. Cover with cling film and marinate in the refrigerator; a couple of hours is fine, overnight is better.

2 Put the peppers in a roasting tin, drizzle with olive oil and vinegar and season. Roast in an oven preheated to 180°C/350°F/gas mark 4 for 45 minutes, until soft. Barely cover the carrots with water and boil until soft. Drain and keep the cooking liquid.

3 Purée the peppers, with the cooking juices, the carrots and cayenne, adding enough carrot cooking liquid to create a smooth purée. Add the cream if using.

4 Cook the lamb, flesh-side down, in an oven preheated to 230°C/450°F/gas mark 8 for 15 minutes, then turn the heat down to 200°C/400°F/gas mark 6 and roast for a further 15 minutes. Cover with foil and a couple of tea towels and leave to rest for 10 minutes. Carve and serve with the purée and a bowl of couscous or bulgar wheat.

For proper *mechoui* lamb, Moroccans cook a whole lamb in a pit with butter and spices until the meat is falling off the bone – not something you can try at home, but this roast still has quite an authentic flavour. It's gorgeous with roast Mediterranean vegetables dressed with shreds of preserved lemon. Even simpler, wrap slices of the lamb and handfuls of salad leaves in warm flatbread and daub with Greek yogurt.

· · · · · ·

mechoui-style lamb

serves 6

1 x 2kg (4½lb) leg of lamb

115g (4oz) unsalted butter, slightly softened

6 garlic cloves, crushed

2 tsp ground cumin

2 tsp ground cayenne

2 tsp ground sweet paprika

salt

I Trim all the fat off the lamb and pull off all the parchment-like white skin. Make deep incisions all over the lamb with a sharp knife. Mash the butter with the garlic and the spices (not salt) and rub it over the lamb, pushing it well down into the holes in the meat. Loosely cover with cling film, put in the refrigerator and leave for about 8 hours, or overnight if you can. Bring to room temperature before roasting.

2 Salt the meat well. Roast in an oven preheated to 220°C/425°F/gas mark 7 for 15 minutes, then turn down to 180°C/350°F/gas mark 4. The lamb needs to cook for another 1¼ hours, slightly longer if you don't want it to be pink. (Proper *mechoui* lamb isn't rare.)

3 Remove the lamb to a warm platter, cover with foil, insulate (I usually use a couple of old towels or tea towels for this) and leave to rest for 15 minutes. Serve the lamb on a big warm platter.

This is adapted from Madhur Jaffrey's *Indian Cookery*, the book that accompanied her first TV series back in the early 1980s. Watching it at home in Northern Ireland – where there were no Indian restaurants and the nearest thing you could get to a curry came in a packet and was made by Vesta – my family was enchanted by this exotic cuisine.

· · · · · ·

indian leg of lamb

serves 6

1 x 2kg (4½lb) leg of lamb

4 tbsp raisins, soaked in boiling water until plump, then drained

15g (½oz) flaked or slivered almonds

marinade

55g (2oz) blanched almonds

2 onions, roughly chopped

8 garlic cloves

a big chunk of fresh root ginger, peeled and roughly chopped

4 green chillies, halved and deseeded

550g (1¼lb) plain yogurt

1 tbsp ground cumin

4 tsp ground coriander

2 tsp ground cinnamon

2 tsp garam masala

salt and pepper (be generous)

1 Trim all the fat off the lamb and pull off all the parchment-like white skin as well. Make deep gashes all over the meat. Put it in a baking dish or roasting tin.

2 Put everything for the marinade into a food processor and blitz. Cover the lamb with it, pushing the marinade down into the cuts in the lamb. Pour the remaining marinade over and around the meat. Cover with cling film and put the lamb into the refrigerator for 24 hours. Turn it every so often if you can.

3 Take the lamb out of the refrigerator and let it come to room temperature. Cover the baking dish or roasting tin with a lid or foil and cook for 1¼ hours in an oven preheated to 200°C/400°F/gas mark 6. Remove the covering and bake for another 30 minutes, basting the lamb a few times. Throw the raisins and the almonds over the lamb and put it back in the oven for another 5 minutes.

4 Leave the cooked lamb to rest for 15 minutes, covered and well insulated with foil and a couple of tea towels over the top. Put the lamb on a warm platter. Skim the excess oil off the top of the cooking juices, then gently reheat them in the pan or roasting tin but don't boil them or the mixture will curdle. Either pour this around the lamb or put it in a bowl or gravy-boat. Serve the lamb immediately

fish

• • • • • •

One-dish cooking seems a difficult proposition when it comes to fish, as it cooks much more quickly than most ingredients. Here the vegetables are half-cooked before the fish is added. These ingredients absolutely sing of the Mediterranean.

· · · · · ·

fish baked with fennel, potatoes and vine tomatoes

serves 4

2 fennel bulbs

600g (1lb 5oz) small waxy potatoes

olive oil

salt and pepper

350g (12oz) vine tomatoes, left on the vine

4 x 300g (10½oz) whole bream or bass, gutted, trimmed and scaled

a handful of flat-leaf parsley, coarsely chopped

juice of ½ lemon

1 Trim the fennel bulbs, reserving the fronds, and remove any tough outer leaves. Quarter and cut out the central core. Cut each piece into slices, about 2mm (⅟₁₆in) thick lengthwise.

2 Cut the potatoes into rounds of the same thickness. Lay the fennel in a roasting tin or large ovenproof serving dish that will take the fish in a single layer. Pour on 1 tbsp olive oil, season and turn the fennel over with your hands, making sure it's well coated. Lay the potatoes on the fennel, season and drizzle with 2 tbsp olive oil. Set the tomatoes on top. Season the tomatoes and drizzle some oil on them, too. Put in an oven preheated to 190°C/375°F/gas mark mark 5.

3 Wash the fish and cut the flesh in three slashes on each side. Season inside and out and put half of the parsley in them.

4 When the vegetables have been cooking for roughly 20 minutes, lay the fish on top of the potatoes and fennel – push the tomatoes out of the way to make room – season, drizzle a little oil on to each fish and put back in the oven. Roast for a further 15 minutes. The fish is cooked when the flesh near the bone is white and opaque.

5 Squeeze the lemon juice over the vegetables and fish, sprinkle on the rest of the parsley and serve immediately.

fish

65

I cook bream a lot. It looks lovely
whole, and has sweet flesh
which nevertheless stands up
to strong flavours.

· · · · · ·

sea bream with lebanese herb sauce

serves 4

4 x 300g (10½oz) sea bream,
gutted, trimmed and scaled

olive oil

salt and pepper

½ tbsp each of finely chopped
flat-leaf parsley and coriander

sauce

115ml (3¾fl oz) extra-virgin
olive oil

1 garlic clove, chopped

1 tsp caster sugar

4 tbsp lemon juice
(almost ½ lemon)

1 tbsp coarsely chopped
flat-leaf parsley

1 tbsp coarsely chopped
mint leaves

2 tbsp coarsely chopped
fresh coriander

1 medium fresh red chilli, halved,
deseeded and chopped

and also...

...with *salmoriglio*

Dissolve 1½ tsp salt in the juice of 2 lemons, add
the chopped leaves of a small bunch of oregano,
whisk in 350ml (12fl oz) extra-virgin olive oil and
season with pepper.

...with black olive, parsley and preserved lemon relish

Mix 300g (10½oz) chopped, pitted black olives,
½ preserved lemon (skin only), finely shredded,
½ finely chopped red onion, a handful of chopped
flat-leaf parsley, 2 finely chopped garlic cloves,
½ chopped red chilli (seeds removed), juice of
½ lemon and 8 tbsp extra-virgin olive oil. Add
pepper and leave for half an hour so that the
flavours can meld.

...with turkish almond *tarator*

Soak 1 slice white bread with about 4 tbsp milk
and leave for half an hour. Purée in a food
processor with 100g (3½oz) blanched almonds,
1 garlic clove, 175ml (6fl oz) extra-virgin olive oil
and the juice of ½ lemon. Add water if you want
a thinner sauce. Season and taste.

I Make three slashes on each side of each fish. Brush the fish inside
and out with olive oil and season all over. Put into an ovenproof
dish or roasting tin and bake for 8 minutes in an oven preheated to
200°C/400°F/gas mark mark 6. Sprinkle with the chopped parsley and
coriander and put back in the oven for a further 5 minutes. The fish is
cooked when the flesh near the bone is white and opaque.

2 Put all the ingredients for the sauce, except the chilli, into a blender
and whiz. Taste for seasoning, then add the chopped chilli. Serve the
fish immediately with the sauce.

As a rough guide, cook whole bream or bass (300g/10½oz) for nine minutes, a 200g/7oz salmon fillet for 12 minutes, and a 200g fillet of cod, haddock or gurnard for 10 minutes, all at 200°C/425°F/gas mark 7.

Sea bass is expensive, so this is a dish for a special occasion (or very dear friends). Despite its simplicity – all you do is stick a fish in the oven – it seems spectacularly luxurious when you open the foil parcel and smell rosemary, fish and wine. I first ate such a dish in Mitchell Tonks' original Fishworks restaurant in Bath, and loved it so much that I recreated it at home. Now it's on the menu whenever I can justify the expense. I like it with olive-oil-roasted potatoes and roast tomatoes.

• • • • • •

roast sea bass with rosemary, garlic and chilli

serves 4

olive oil

1 sea bass, 1.5kg (3lb 5oz), gutted and scaled

salt and pepper

3 rosemary sprigs

2 dried red chillies, crumbled

2 garlic bulbs, cloves separated but not peeled

85ml (3fl oz) dry white wine

I Lay a large piece of foil in a roasting tin or on a baking sheet – it should be big enough to come up in a 'tent' around the fish – and lightly oil the centre. Put the sea bass on top, season inside and out and tuck a couple of sprigs of rosemary inside. Scatter the chilli and the leaves from the last sprig of rosemary on top of the fish. Throw the cloves of garlic around it and drizzle some olive oil over the top.

2 Pull the foil up around the fish and pour on the wine. Pull the sides of the foil together and scrunch the edges to make a tent around the fish. It must *not* be wrapped tightly in the foil because the fish needs space to steam. Cook in an oven preheated to 200°C/400°F/gas mark 6 for 30 minutes. Serve from the foil tent in which the fish has cooked.

Don't be fooled by the simplicity of this recipe. Fish baked with a crust can be really disappointing. (If you've tasted the many ready-meal versions you'll know what I mean.) But abundant lemon zest and chopped parsley make this crust fresh and zingy.

. . . . . .

baked cod with a zesty crust

serves 4

1 slice white bread (about 40g/1½oz), with no crusts

20g (¾oz) flat-leaf parsley

40g (1½oz) Parmesan, freshly grated

2 garlic cloves, finely chopped

finely grated rind of 1 unwaxed lemon

a good squeeze of lemon juice

7 tbsp olive oil

salt and pepper

4 x 200g (7oz) Icelandic cod, or gurnard, fillets

I Put the bread and parsley in a food processor and whiz. Tip into a bowl and add the cheese, garlic, lemon rind and juice, 5 tbsp of the oil and seasoning.

2 Drizzle the rest of the oil onto a baking sheet. Turn the fillets over in the oil to coat them on both sides. Leave flesh-side up and pat the crumbs on top. Put into an oven preheated to 220ºC/425ºF/gas mark 7 and cook for 7-10 minutes, depending on the thickness of the fish. Transfer to hot plates to serve.

Frying to get a good golden colour, then finishing in the oven is a hassle-free way to cook fish fillets. It's even simpler if you have a frying or sauté pan that can go in the oven. If not, just transfer the fish to a roasting tin. This dish is lovely with pea purée (page 25).

. . . . . .

roast cod with smoked bacon

serves 2

3 tbsp olive oil

salt and pepper

2 x 200g (7oz) Icelandic cod, or gurnard, fillets

200g (7oz) smoked bacon lardons

35g (1¼oz) unsalted butter

a squeeze of lemon juice

1 tbsp finely chopped flat-leaf parsley

I Heat 2 tbsp of olive oil in a frying pan that can go in the oven. Season the cod and put it, flesh-side down, into the pan. Cook for about 1½ minutes, until lightly browned underneath. Turn it over and pop the pan into an oven preheated to 220ºC/425ºF/gas mark 7 for 7-10 minutes, depending on the thickness of the fillets.

2 While the fish is roasting, heat the rest of the olive oil in a small frying pan and cook the bacon until it is browned on all sides. Add the butter and melt until foaming. Add the juice and parsley. Pour the buttery bacon and parsley over the cod. Serve immediately.

A classy dish, which succeeds because of the interplay of flavours — the sweetness of cod, the saltiness of anchovies and the earthiness of beans. Chopped black olives can be added to the anchovy dressing (in which case add more lemon and olive oil) or replace the anchovies altogether.

· · · · · ·

roast cod with anchovies and bean purée

serves 4

1 x 50g can cured anchovies, drained of oil

1 tbsp chopped flat-leaf parsley

6 tbsp extra-virgin olive oil

a good squeeze of lemon

2 tbsp olive oil

salt and pepper

4 x 175g (6oz) Icelandic cod, or gurnard, fillets

beans

2 tbsp olive oil

½ onion, roughly chopped

1 garlic clove, crushed

2 x 410g cans cannellini beans, drained

150ml (5fl oz) chicken stock or water

4 tbsp extra-virgin olive oil

a good squeeze of lemon

I For the beans, heat the olive oil in a saucepan and gently cook the onion until it is soft but not coloured. Add the garlic, the beans, stock or water and seasoning. Cook over a medium heat for about 4 minutes.

2 Process the beans and the liquid in a blender or food processor with the extra-virgin olive oil and the lemon juice. Taste and adjust the seasoning. You can set the purée aside to heat up later, or serve it at room temperature.

3 Chop the anchovies and parsley together and stir in the extra-virgin olive oil. Add a squeeze of lemon as well. Keep until you need it.

4 Heat the 2 tbsp olive oil in a non-stick frying pan over a medium-high heat. Lightly season the cod and cook, skin-side down first, for 2 minutes, then turn the cod over and cook for another minute. The fillets should be a nice gold colour on both sides. Transfer the fillets to a roasting tin and cook in an oven preheated to 200°C/400°F/gas mark 6 for about 8 minutes; by then the fish should be opaque and cooked through, but still moist.

5 Serve the fish with the bean purée and some of the anchovy dressing spooned over the top.

We're nervous about cooking fish, but get the cooking times for several varieties (of a certain size) in your head and it can be as easy as grilling a chop.

serves 4

500g (18oz) smoked haddock fillet

200ml (7fl oz) milk

15g (½oz) unsalted butter, plus extra for buttering

250g (9oz) tomatoes, halved

salt and pepper

200ml (7fl oz) double cream

100g (3½oz) mature Cheddar, grated

A perfect supper dish for an autumn or winter evening. Instead of the tomatoes, you can serve buttered leeks, sliced and sweated for about 15 minutes, or broccoli which you've cooked until just tender; purple-sprouting broccoli is especially good. I sometimes spread a little grain mustard over the fish before adding the vegetables and cream.

. . . . . .

scottish smokies

I Put the haddock in a pan with the milk. Bring the milk up to the boil, then quickly turn the heat down low. Cover with a lid and poach the fish for 5 minutes; it should be only just cooked. Remove the skin from the fish and transfer the fish to a buttered gratin dish.

2 Scoop the insides from the tomatoes and discard. Cut the flesh into slices. Melt the butter in a frying pan and quickly sauté the tomatoes until they are softening. Season. Increase the heat to reduce the tomato cooking juices – you don't want the tomatoes to be too wet.

3 Spoon the tomatoes onto the fish. Pour on the cream and top with the grated cheese. Bake in an oven preheated to 190ºC/375ºF/gas mark 5 for 20 minutes. Serve golden and bubbling.

A dish I first ate in Sweden, where they're fond of oily fish. If you can't get wild mushrooms, use cultivated field mushrooms rather than button mushrooms as they have a much better flavour. Cut the field mushrooms into slices about 5mm (¼in) thick.

. . . . . .

mackerel fillets with mushrooms, parsley and lemon

serves 4

8 mackerel fillets

salt and pepper

45g (1½oz) unsalted butter

125g (4½oz) mushrooms, preferably a mixture of fresh wild ones and shiitake or oyster

a good squeeze of lemon juice

a small handful of flat-leaf parsley, finely chopped

lemon wedges, to serve

I Season the mackerel on both sides and melt 15g (½oz) of the butter in a non-stick frying pan. Fry the fillets, flesh-side down first, until golden, then carefully turn over and cook on the skin-side until crisp and golden. It will take about 3 minutes on each side to cook them through. Remove and keep warm while you quickly cook the mushrooms.

2 Cut any large mushrooms in half or quarters. Add the rest of the butter to the mackerel pan, turn the heat up and briskly sauté the mushrooms until they are golden. Add salt, pepper, a good squeeze of lemon and the parsley. Serve the mushrooms spooned over or beside the mackerel. Provide lemon wedges.

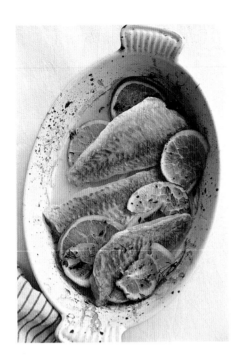

An utterly simple and lovely dish. To make it with fillets of mullet instead of whole fish, cook the fruit with the oil and thyme for 10 minutes, then add eight good-sized fillets and the olives and spoon some of the fruit juices and olive oil over the top. Season and cook for another eight minutes.

· · · · · ·

greek red mullet with oranges and olives

serves 4

salt and pepper

4 large red mullet, about 225g (8oz) each, cleaned and gutted

a good handful of thyme sprigs

4 tbsp olive oil, plus a little extra for drizzling

juice of ½ lemon

1 large orange (thin-skinned if possible)

4 tbsp stoned black olives

I Season the mullet inside and out and stuff some of the thyme sprigs inside the fish. Put the fish in an ovenproof dish where they can lie in a single layer.

2 Mix the olive oil with the lemon juice and the juice of ½ of the orange and pour this all over the fish. Cut the rest of the orange into thin slices, halve these and tuck them around the fish with the rest of the thyme. Season and drizzle on a little more olive oil.

3 Bake in an oven preheated to 180°C/350°F/gas mark 4 for 15 minutes. Add the black olives and put the fish back in the oven for another 10 minutes.

fish

Tuna is a very satisfying, meaty fish. If you cook it to be slightly rare in the middle, it can be ready in minutes. This tuna goes well with corn cakes, to pick up on the Mexican theme, or with olive-oil-and-garlic-roasted potatoes.

• • • • • •

seared tuna with avocado salsa

serves 4

4 thick tuna loin steaks

olive oil

salt and pepper

salsa

2 avocados, peeled and chopped

200g (7oz) tomatoes, finely chopped

1 tsp ground cumin

2 garlic cloves, finely chopped

2 spring onions, finely chopped

2 medium red chillies, deseeded and finely chopped

juice of ½ lime

2 tbsp chopped fresh coriander

4 tbsp extra-virgin olive oil

Tabasco sauce, to taste (optional)

to serve

1 small tub sour cream

coriander leaves

2 limes

and also...

...with capers, chilli and lemon

Cook 2 thick tuna loin steaks as in the main recipe. Keep warm while you make the dressing. Gently heat 3 tbsp extra-virgin olive oil in a small frying pan. Add 2 sliced garlic cloves, a medium red chilli, halved, deseeded and very finely sliced, and 2 tbsp rinsed capers and cook for about 30 seconds over a low heat. Add a handful of chopped flat-leaf parsley, the zest of ½ unwaxed lemon and plenty of lemon juice. Taste and season if necessary. Pour some dressing over each piece of fish and serve immediately.

...with warm beans and salsa verde

Make the salsa verde by following the recipe on page 111. Heat 2 tbsp olive oil in a frying pan and sauté 1 finely sliced onion until soft but not coloured. Add a crushed garlic clove and cook for another minute, then add a drained 410g (14½oz) can of cannellini beans and another 2 tbsp of olive oil. Season and let the beans heat through. Finish with a squeeze of lemon juice and a handful of chopped flat-leaf parsley. Check the seasoning. Cook 2 tuna loin steaks as in the main recipe and serve on the beans with the salsa verde.

I Mix all the salsa ingredients together, but don't do it more than an hour ahead of serving as it discolours. Add extra hot pepper sauce if you want it to be a little spicier. Once you've made it, cover the salsa and let the flavours infuse.

2 Use a cast-iron griddle for cooking the fish, if you've got one. Brush each piece of tuna with a little oil and season well on both sides. Let the griddle pan get very hot, then cook the tuna for 1½ minutes on each side so that it's still pink in the middle, like a very rare steak.

3 Serve the tuna with a generous spoonful of salsa and a dollop of sour cream alongside. Top with a sprig of coriander and add half a lime to each plate.

Make the sauce for this ahead of time if you want to, then cook the tuna at the last minute.

. . . . . .

sicilian sweet-and-sour tuna

Tuna is a brilliant fish for meat-eaters. Quickly seared on the outside and left rare in the middle, it's as satisfying as steak, and no more difficult to cook. And you get a classy meal in minutes.

serves 6

10 tbsp olive oil

2 large onions, finely sliced

3 celery stalks, very finely sliced

125g (4½oz) raisins, soaked in hot water and drained

175ml (6fl oz) white-wine vinegar

250ml (9fl oz) Marsala

75g (2¾oz) green olives

2 tbsp caster sugar

salt and pepper

6 tuna loin steaks, 1-1.5cm (½-⅝in) thick

25g (1oz) mint leaves, torn into shreds

extra-virgin olive oil, to serve

I Heat 6 tbsp of the olive oil in a sauté pan and add the onions and celery. Cook, stirring occasionally, for about 10 minutes, until the onions are golden and soft. Then add the raisins, vinegar, Marsala, olives and sugar and season. Stir to combine, let the mixture cook for a couple of minutes and taste for seasoning – the mixture should be sweet-sour, but you need to get the balance right and may want to adjust it by adding more vinegar or sugar.

2 Brush the tuna steaks on both sides with the rest of the olive oil and season with salt and pepper. Heat a ridged griddle pan, or an ordinary frying pan, until really hot. Quickly sear the tuna on both sides so that it gets a good colour. Transfer the tuna to the sauté pan and cook for a couple of minutes in the 'sauce' that you have already made. Sicilians like the tuna in this dish to be cooked through, but I still prefer it slightly raw in the middle, so cook according to your taste.

3 Add the mint leaves and serve, with a slug of extra-virgin olive oil on top.

This recipe is a boon. Pick the ingredients up on the way home from work and you'll have a lovely summery dish on the table in 20 minutes. You can add herbs – chervil or parsley, for example – to the sauce, and serve it with cold salmon or roast chicken as well.

. . . . . .

salmon en papillote with watercress sauce

serves 4

4 x 200g (7oz) salmon fillets

salt and pepper

55g (2oz) butter, melted

½ medium onion, very finely sliced

1 lemon

8 dill sprigs

4 tbsp dry vermouth

sauce

150g (5½oz) fromage frais

150g (5½oz) good-quality mayonnaise

75g (2¾oz) watercress

I Cut out four rectangles of greaseproof paper. Each rectangle should be able to hold one salmon fillet comfortably, with enough paper to fold around it generously to make a parcel.

2 Season the fish well. Brush the middle of each rectangle with melted butter and divide the onion slices among them. Drizzle the onions with a little more butter, season, then put the fillets on top. Squeeze some lemon and put 2 sprigs of dill on each fillet. Sprinkle on the vermouth and divide the remaining melted butter among the parcels.

3 To make each parcel, pull the two longest sides of the greaseproof paper up around the salmon and fold. Keep folding this until the parcel is firmly sealed at the top, but there is plenty of room round the salmon for steam to circulate. Twist the ends of each parcel as if it were a cracker. Place on a metal baking sheet and bake in an oven preheated to 200°C/400°F/gas mark 6 for 12 minutes.

4 Make the sauce by whizzing the ingredients in a blender or food processor. Season.

5 When the salmon is cooked, you can either open the parcels slightly to reveal the contents, or let the diners do this. The sauce is lovely spooned into the parcel, where it mixes with the cooking juices. Serve the rest on the side.

fish

The sauce is a classic, which is also delicious with whole baked salmon or roast chicken.

· · · · · ·

salmon fillets with sauce messine

serves 4

4 x 200g (7oz) salmon fillets

sauce

15g (½oz) butter

1 shallot, very finely chopped

½ tsp plain flour

175ml (6fl oz) double cream

1 tsp Dijon mustard

½ tbsp each of finely chopped parsley and chervil leaves from 2 stems tarragon, chopped

juice of ½ lemon

salt and pepper

1 Brush a baking sheet with a little oil and lay the salmon fillets on it, skin-side down. Cook in an oven preheated to 200°C/400°F/gas mark 6 for 12 minutes.

2 Meanwhile, melt the butter in a small pan and sauté the shallot until soft. Stir in the flour and cook for a minute. Take off the heat and gradually beat in the cream. Return to the heat and gently bring to the boil. Add the other ingredients and simmer for 2-3 minutes, until you can taste the herbs. Adjust the flavour and consistency as necessary. Serve warm.

A brilliantly easy recipe, loosely adapted from a Swedish one in Mark Hix's column in *The Independent*.

· · · · · ·

baked salmon with mustard and honey

serves 4

a little sunflower or groundnut oil

4 x 175g (6oz) salmon fillets

2 tbsp grain mustard

2 tbsp runny honey

½ tbsp chopped dill

1 Brush a baking sheet with a little oil and lay the salmon fillets on it, skin-side down. Mix the mustard, honey and dill together and spoon it over the fish. Roast in an oven preheated to 200°C/400°F/ gas mark 6 for 12 minutes.

2 Serve immediately with baby new potatoes and a cucumber salad.

Flavoured butters are probably the easiest way to dress up grilled fish and meat. Just pound soft butter in a mortar or beat everything together with a wooden spoon until thoroughly blended. Chill, then shape into a cylinder and wrap in cling film. Most will keep in the refrigerator for 2–3 days.

. . . .

flavoured butters

herb butter
Pound 75g (2¾oz) butter with 3 tbsp finely chopped herbs – a mixture of chervil, basil, parsley – until combined. Good with nearly anything grilled.

juniper and thyme butter
Pound 75g (2¾oz) butter with 1 tbsp juniper berries, the juice of ½ small lemon and the leaves from 4 sprigs of thyme. Most delicious with pork chops.

prawn butter
Pound 75g (2¾oz) butter with 2 tbsp finely chopped chervil, dill or parsley and the juice of ½ small lemon. Finely chop 55g (2oz) cooked prawns and blend these in without squashing them too much. You can also replace the prawns with chopped smoked salmon trimmings. Eat within 24 hours.

mint and cider butter
Pound 75g (2¾oz) butter with 2 tbsp chopped mint, 1 tsp caster sugar, salt and pepper. Gradually beat in 1 tbsp cider vinegar. Serve with grilled lamb.

dill butter
Pound 75g (2¾oz) butter with 2 tbsp very finely chopped pickled dill cucumber and 3 tbsp chopped dill. Lovely melted over warm salmon.

martini butter
Pound 75g (2¾oz) butter with 3 tbsp chopped chervil and chives, then gradually add 1 tbsp dry vermouth. Delicious with grilled Mediterranean fish.

roquefort butter
Pound 75g (2¾oz) unsalted butter with 50g (1¾oz) crumbled Roquefort. A classic with steak, but good, too, with grilled chicken.

tomato and smoked paprika butter
Pound 75g (2¾oz) butter with 25g (1oz) roughly chopped sun-blush tomatoes, 1 small crushed garlic clove, 1½ tsp smoked paprika and freshly ground pepper. These great Spanish flavours work best with pork, chicken and grilled Mediterranean fish.

black olive and anchovy butter
Pound 75g (2¾oz) unsalted butter with 3 drained, chopped anchovy fillets, 1 crushed garlic clove and a squeeze of lemon juice. Carefully mix in the chopped flesh of 25g (1oz) good-quality black olives. Try with meaty fish, chicken and lamb.

basil and tomato butter
Pound 75g (2¾oz) butter with about 24 torn basil leaves, 25g (1oz) roughly chopped sun-blush tomatoes, 1 crushed garlic clove and freshly ground pepper. Works well with both chicken and fish.

chilli and coriander butter
Pound 75g (2¾oz) butter with about 4 heaped tbsp finely chopped fresh coriander, 1 crushed garlic clove, the zest and juice of ½ lime, salt and pepper. Mix in 1 medium fresh red chilli, halved, deseeded and finely chopped. Works brilliantly with nearly everything, including hot corn on the cob.

pasta

Pasta *is* convenient. Nests of dried tagliatelle can sit happily in the cupboard for years. Pasta's quick to cook and, since you only need a fork, it can be eaten in front of the telly, on the floor or in bed. But it has to be prepared with care.

This is my standby pasta dish. I always have the ingredients for it and I often prefer it to something more complicated. Its simplicity is very satisfying.

· · · · · ·

spaghetti with parsley, chilli and garlic

serves 4

175g (6oz) spaghetti

salt and pepper

3 tbsp extra-virgin olive oil

2 garlic cloves, sliced

1 tsp dried chilli flakes

juice of ½ lemon

a generous handful of flat-leaf parsley (about 10g/¼oz), finely chopped

I Cook the pasta in plenty of boiling salted water until *al dente*. While it's cooking, heat the oil in a large frying pan and sauté the garlic and chilli for 1–1½ minutes. The garlic should be pale gold. Drain the pasta and immediately add to the frying pan. Season, add the lemon juice and parsley, and heat for about 30 seconds.

and also...

...spaghetti with anchovies, parsley and vermouth
Cook ½ chopped onion and 3 sliced garlic cloves in 4 tbsp olive oil until soft. Add 100g can anchovies (drained). Press the anchovies with a wooden spoon to help them disintegrate, then turn up the heat and add 2 tbsp vermouth, pepper, a handful of chopped parsley, some lemon, a slug of extra-virgin olive oil and toss with cooked, drained spaghetti.

Somehow, although this dish takes no more effort than bacon and eggs, it elevates those very ordinary ingredients.

• • • • • •

spaghetti with bacon, egg and smoked cheese

serves 2

175g (6oz) spaghetti

salt and pepper

3 tbsp olive oil

125g (4½oz) bacon lardons

2 large eggs

2 tbsp extra-virgin olive oil

1 tbsp coarsely chopped flat-leaf parsley

55g (2oz) smoked cheese, grated

I Cook the spaghetti in plenty of boiling salted water until *al dente*. When it's almost ready, heat 1 tbsp olive oil in a large frying pan and cook the lardons until they're cooked and well coloured. Tip them into a bowl and heat the rest of the oil. Fry the eggs, spooning the warm oil up over the top of the eggs to cook the yolks. Season.

2 Drain the pasta, then put it back in the saucepan. Add the extra-virgin olive oil, pepper, a little salt, the bacon and parsley and toss. Divide between two plates, sprinkle on the grated cheese and top each serving with a fried egg. Serve immediately.

The combination of sweet onions, blue cheese and walnuts is irresistible.

• • • • • •

penne with roasted onions, gorgonzola and walnuts

serves 4

3 large onions, peeled and halved

6 tbsp olive oil

2 tbsp balsamic vinegar

salt and pepper

300g (10½oz) penne or other pasta shapes

100g (3½oz) Gorgonzola cheese, crumbled

3 tbsp coarsely chopped flat-leaf parsley

75g (2¾oz) toasted walnut pieces

5 tbsp extra-virgin olive oil

I Cut each onion half into crescent-shaped slices, about 1.5cm (⅝in) thick. Toss in a roasting tin with the olive oil, balsamic and seasoning. Roast at 190°C/375°F/gas mark mark 5 for 30–35 minutes, shaking the tin every so often. The onions should be tender and slightly charred.

2 Cook the pasta, drain and return it to the saucepan. Add the onions and the rest of the ingredients. Stir and serve.

Good in autumn and winter when basil and pine nuts seem too summery. You can toss torn rocket or baby spinach leaves with the hot pasta before adding the sauce if you want a more substantial dish (or you're trying to boost your intake of greens).

· · · · · ·

pappardelle with ligurian walnut sauce

Like everyone, I turn to pasta when there isn't much food in the house. "What about pasta?" I murmur indifferently. Then I'll feel a little rise of pleasure as I spot some parsley, which can be tossed with spaghetti, extra-virgin olive oil and chilli, or some dried wild mushrooms, which can be soaked and cooked with cream to dress broad strands of tagliatelle.

serves 4

300g (10½oz) pappardelle

salt and pepper

a bunch of flat-leaf parsley (about 30g/1¼oz), coarsely chopped

ligurian walnut sauce

25g (1oz – about 1 slice) coarse bread

100g (3½oz) shelled walnuts

1 garlic clove

75ml (2½fl oz) olive oil

125ml (4fl oz) double cream

55g (2oz) Parmesan, freshly grated

I Soak the bread in a little water for 10 minutes or so, then squeeze out the excess. Put this into a mortar or a food processor with the walnuts and garlic and pound or blend. Stir in the olive oil, cream, Parmesan and seasoning. You should have a thick, creamy sauce.

2 Cook the pappardelle in plenty of boiling salted water until *al dente.* Mix 2 tbsp of the pasta-cooking water with the sauce, then drain the pasta. Toss the pasta with the sauce and the parsley and serve immediately.

serves 2

150g (5½oz) black pasta, either spaghetti or linguine

salt and pepper

400g (14oz) squid, cleaned and prepared

4 tbsp olive oil

6 garlic cloves, sliced

1 red chilli, halved, deseeded and finely shredded

1 tbsp chopped flat-leaf parsley

juice of ½ lemon

4 tbsp extra-virgin olive oil

I Cook the pasta in plenty of boiling salted water until *al dente*. While it's cooking, wash the squid, making sure to remove any gunge from inside the bodies, and pat dry. Cut the wings from the main body. If the squid are large, slice these wings in three or four strips, then cut the body in half lengthwise and cut the halves into strips about 1cm (½in) thick. If the squid are small, you need only cut off the little wings and then slice the whole body into rings, again about 1cm (½in) thick.

2 When the pasta is almost ready, heat the olive oil in a large frying pan or wok – the oil must get really hot. Stir-fry the squid for about 40 seconds, then turn the heat down a little and add the garlic and chilli. Cook for another 30 seconds or so. (The garlic should go pale golden; be careful not to burn it.) Throw in the parsley, squeeze on the lemon and season. Quickly drain the pasta and toss it with the extra-virgin olive oil and the squid. Serve immediately.

Black pasta looks sensational – very dramatic – so it's good to have a packet in the cupboard. You can make this with king prawns instead of squid and use chilli flakes if you don't have a fresh chilli.

· · · · · ·

black pasta with squid, chilli and garlic

Warm pasta, soft ricotta and sweet vegetables make a wonderful interplay of textures, temperatures and flavours in your mouth.

. . . . . .

trofie with bacon, peas, ricotta and mint

serves 4

350g (12oz) *trofie* or other pasta shapes

salt and pepper

300g (10½oz) bacon lardons

4 tbsp olive oil

225g (8oz) frozen peas

35g (1¼oz) fresh mint leaves, torn

250g (9oz) ricotta cheese (fresh if possible), roughly broken up

4 tbsp extra-virgin olive oil

freshly grated Parmesan, for serving

I Cook the pasta in plenty of boiling salted water until *al dente*. While the pasta is cooking, fry the bacon in the olive oil until it is cooked and golden on all sides. Add the peas and about 50ml (2fl oz) water and cook until the peas are tender and the water has disappeared. Season.

2 Drain the pasta and toss it with the bacon, peas and mint. Gently fork in the ricotta, drizzle with the extra-virgin olive oil, season again and serve with freshly grated Parmesan.

Prawns and feta might seem strange bedfellows, but they work very well (as Greeks know). This is a really bright, summery dish.

. . . . . .

trofie with prawns, feta, parsley and lemon

serves 4

300g (10½oz) *trofie* or other pasta shapes

salt and pepper

1kg (2¼lb) raw shelled prawns

4 tbsp olive oil

3 garlic cloves, finely chopped

finely grated zest of 1 unwaxed lemon

juice of ½ lemon

150g (5½oz) feta cheese, crumbled

4 tbsp roughly chopped flat-leaf parsley

4 tbsp extra-virgin olive oil

I Cook the pasta in plenty of boiling salted water until *al dente*. While it's cooking, sauté the prawns for about 2 minutes in the olive oil, then add the garlic and cook for another minute. Throw in the lemon zest and juice and some pepper.

2 Drain the pasta, return it to the pan and gently mix the prawns into it along with all the other ingredients. Serve immediately.

You can use a bought tub of stock for this, but add some dry Marsala or white wine if you do that, as commercial stock tends to have a less-rich flavour than home-made.

• • • • • •

tagliatelle with wild mushroom sauce

serves 4

15g (½oz) dried wild mushrooms

15g (½oz) butter

75g (2¾oz) cultivated mushrooms, cleaned and roughly chopped

350ml (12fl oz) well-flavoured chicken stock

125ml (4fl oz) double cream

salt and pepper

450g (1lb) tagliatelle

freshly grated Parmesan, for serving

I Pour boiling water over the dried mushrooms and leave to soak for 15 minutes. Melt the butter and sauté the other mushrooms until well coloured. Drain the wild mushrooms, reserving the soaking liquor. Add to the pan and cook for a minute. Pour on the chicken stock and the soaking liquor and cook until the liquid is reduced by two-thirds. Add the cream and simmer until the sauce coats the back of a spoon. Taste and season.

2 Cook the pasta in boiling salted water, drain and dress with the sauce. Serve with grated Parmesan.

Simple but somehow luxurious – I think it's the abundance of lemon. You can use flakes of cooked salmon instead of Parma ham, and add asparagus when it's in season.

• • • • • •

tagliatelle with lemon, parma ham and peas

serves 4

275ml (9½fl oz) double cream

finely grated zest of 4 unwaxed lemons

juice of 1½ lemons

350g (12oz) tagliatelle

salt and pepper

300g (10½oz) frozen or fresh peas (podded weight)

55g (2oz) Parmesan, grated, plus more for serving

175g (6oz) Parma ham, torn into strips about 1.5cm (⅝in) wide

a small bunch of chervil, coarsely chopped

I Put the cream and the lemon zest and juice into a sauté pan and bring to the boil. Reduce by a third (be careful: it reduces very quickly). Cook the tagliatelle in plenty of boiling salted water until *al dente*, and cook the peas until just tender.

2 Add the peas, Parmesan and seasoning to the cream. Drain the pasta and add it to the pan along with the ham and the chervil. Heat everything through gently for about 20 seconds and serve immediately with extra grated Parmesan.

serves 4

325g (11½oz) tagliatelle

salt

400g (14oz) hot-smoked salmon

25g (1oz) unsalted butter

4 tbsp vodka or dry white wine

300ml (10fl oz) sour cream

4 tbsp chopped dill

freshly ground black pepper

4 heaped tsp *keta* (salmon caviar)

Good for a mid-week supper with friends before or after a cinema trip. The salmon caviar makes it special, but you can leave it out (it's expensive). Add cooked peas or little spears of asparagus when they're in season. You can use smoked trout instead of salmon, or a mixture of smoked and fresh cooked salmon.

• • • • • •

tagliatelle with hot-smoked salmon, sour cream and vodka

I Cook the tagliatelle in plenty of boiling salted water until *al dente*. While it's cooking, break the hot-smoked salmon into flakes, discarding the skin. Melt the butter in a frying pan and add the salmon. Cook for about a minute, then add the vodka or wine. Continue to cook until most of the alcohol has evaporated. Add the sour cream and heat through, but don't allow it to boil. Add the dill and pepper (you shouldn't need salt as the salmon and the *keta* are salty).

2 Drain the pasta and add it to the sauce in the pan. Toss everything together, then divide among four warm plates or bowls. Put a spoonful of *keta* on the top of each serving.

I find normal basil pesto just a little cloying, so I like the tartness goat cheese brings. It might seem like a strange combination, but this is also good with sautéed strips of bitter radicchio instead of tomatoes.

· · · · · ·

fettuccine with goat-cheese pesto and roast tomatoes

serves 4

24 cherry tomatoes (about 450g/1lb)

2 tbsp olive oil

salt and pepper

350g (12oz) fettuccine

goat-cheese pesto

75g (2¾oz) basil leaves

35g (1¼oz) pine nuts

2 garlic cloves

35g (1¼oz) Parmesan, freshly grated

salt and pepper

175ml (6fl oz) extra-virgin olive oil

100g (3½oz) soft goat cheese

I Put the tomatoes in a roasting tin, drizzle with the olive oil and season. Roast in an oven preheated to 190°C/375°F/gas mark 5 until they are completely soft and a little charred – about 20–25 minutes. They can be either hot or at room temperature when added to the pasta.

2 Put the basil, pine nuts, garlic, half the Parmesan and salt and pepper into a food processor. Blend, gradually adding the olive oil, then stir in the rest of the Parmesan. Break the goat cheese up and gently stir it into the pesto. Check the seasoning.

3 Cook the fettuccine in plenty of boiling salted water until *al dente*. Drain and toss in a warmed bowl with the pesto and the roast tomatoes.

leaves
and
herbs

Georgian cooking is full of walnuts, pomegranates and coriander. They're unfamiliar to our taste buds, but wonderful in combination, and very pretty to look at.

· · · · · ·

georgian aubergine salad with walnuts, pomegranates and coriander

serves 4

3 aubergines

olive oil

salt and pepper

250g (9oz) Greek yogurt

55g (2oz) walnut pieces, toasted

100g (3½oz) coriander leaves

seeds from 1 pomegranate

dressing

1½ tbsp pomegranate molasses

2 garlic cloves, crushed

1 medium red chilli, halved, deseeded and very finely sliced

1 tsp runny honey (or according to taste)

a really good squeeze of lemon juice

5 tbsp extra-virgin olive oil

I Trim the ends off the aubergines and cut them lengthwise into slices about 8mm (⅜in) thick. Toss the slices in a bowl (you can do this in batches) with olive oil, salt and pepper. Be generous: the slices should be well coated. Put them on baking sheets and roast for about 25 minutes in an oven preheated to 200ºC/400ºF/gas mark mark 6. The aubergines should be golden and soft. (You can fry the aubergines if you prefer, but it means more time standing at the cooker.)

2 To make the dressing, mix salt, pepper and everything else (except the oil) together in a cup, then whisk in the olive oil with a fork. Taste for seasoning. Aubergine is quite bland, so it can take a strongly flavoured dressing.

3 Pour two-thirds of the dressing over the warm aubergines and leave them to soak it up if you have time.

4 To assemble the salad, layer the aubergines in a broad shallow bowl with the yogurt, walnuts, coriander leaves and seasoning. Scatter the pomegranate seeds over the top and drizzle with the rest of the dressing.

leaves and herbs

serves 4 as a main course

1kg (2¼lb) butternut squash

3 tbsp olive oil

salt and pepper

1 tsp caster sugar

1 red chilli, halved, deseeded and finely shredded

150g (5½oz) salad leaves (I like a mixture of baby spinach and watercress)

150g (5½oz) feta cheese, broken into chunks

30g (1¼oz) pitted black olives

dressing

1½ tsp white-wine vinegar

a smidgen of Dijon mustard

5 tbsp extra-virgin olive oil

a generous pinch of caster sugar

Roast squash is great in winter salads; it's a good, meaty ingredient with a wonderful colour. It's also much less hassle to prepare than you might expect: you don't even have to peel the slices because the skin becomes so soft during roasting. This dish is a great mixture of sweet and salty flavours.

· · · · · ·

roast squash, feta and black olive salad

I Halve the squash and remove the seeds. Cut into slices lengthwise (about 1.5cm/⅝in wide at the thickest part) and put on a metal baking tray. Drizzle with the olive oil, and sprinkle with salt, pepper and the sugar. Turn over with your hands, making sure the squash gets well coated. Put into an oven preheated to 200°C/400°F/ gas mark 6, and roast for 25 minutes. Scatter the chilli over the squash in the last 10 minutes of cooking time. Leave the squash to cool a little.

2 Make the dressing by putting the vinegar, mustard and some salt and pepper into a cup then whisking in the oil with a fork. Add a little sugar, then taste and adjust the seasoning if you need to.

3 Toss the leaves with two-thirds of the dressing in a broad, shallow bowl, then put the rest of the salad ingredients on top. Drizzle on the remaining dressing.

Figs are luxurious and sexy, so perfect for making a salad seem special. You could use a blue cheese instead of the goat cheese, or substitute smoked duck or warm duck breast for the cheese.

· · · · · ·

goat cheese and fig salad

serves 4

12 figs, cut in half, brushed with olive oil and sprinkled with a little caster sugar

200g (7oz) salad leaves: baby spinach, watercress or lamb's lettuce, or a mixture

55g (2oz) shelled hazelnuts, halved and toasted

200g (7oz) goat cheese, broken into chunks

dressing

a smidgen of Dijon mustard

salt and pepper

1½ tbsp red-wine vinegar

1 tsp crème de cassis (blackcurrant liqueur)

2 tbsp olive oil and 6 tbsp hazelnut oil

I For the dressing, shake all the ingredients together in a jam jar. Check the seasoning.

2 Heat a ridged griddle pan over a medium heat and cook the figs, cut-side down, for about 3 minutes, until soft and caramelized.

3 Toss the leaves and nuts with most of the dressing, then arrange the figs and cheese on top. Drizzle with the rest of the dressing and serve.

This recipe is adapted from one in a book called *Verdura* by Viana La Place (published by Grub Street), which makes me want to eat vegetables all the time. Who can resist a dish with such a name?

· · · · · ·

dama bianca

serves 4

450g (1lb) fresh mozzarella cheese

2 fennel bulbs

2 white celery stalks, plus any leaves attached

salt and pepper

juice of 1 lemon

100ml (3½fl oz) extra-virgin olive oil

shavings of Parmesan or pecorino cheese (optional)

I Drain the mozzarella and dry with kitchen paper.

2 Cut off any feathery bits on the fennel and save them. Halve each bulb and trim the base. Slice each half thinly with a sharp knife, or a mandolin if you have one. Trim the celery stalks and cut into fine (julienne) strips. Tear the celery leaves very roughly.

3 Cut the mozzarella into thin slices and arrange on a platter or individual plates, interleaving them with the fennel, celery and celery leaves. Season with salt, pepper and lemon juice as you go, and drizzle with olive oil. Snip any feathery bits of fennel over the top. Scatter on the Parmesan (if using) and finish with a drizzle of olive oil.

Always on the menu in a raffish Parisian bistro called *Le Petit Gavroche*, where I used to eat as a teenager, this is still one of my favourite salads.

· · · · · ·

salade gavrocharde

serves 4

125g (4½oz) salad leaves (I like frisée and baby spinach)

12 well-flavoured tomatoes, quartered

55g (2oz) walnut pieces, toasted

125g (4½oz) Roquefort cheese, crumbled

dressing

1 tsp white-wine vinegar

a smidgen of Dijon mustard

salt and pepper

a pinch of caster sugar

4 tbsp extra-virgin olive oil

I Make the dressing by whisking all the ingredients together with a fork. Toss the salad ingredients with the dressing and serve immediately.

and also...

...salade de nevers
Make the salad as above, adding 150g (5½oz) sautéed bacon lardons and topping each serving with a poached egg.

A French bistro classic. The walnuts can be replaced with hazelnuts and the Roquefort with Cashel Blue or Gorgonzola.

· · · · · ·

pear, roquefort and walnut salad

serves 2

2 small ripe pears, halved and cored

lemon juice, if necessary

55g (2oz) walnut halves

100g (3½oz) salad leaves (a mixture of watercress and white chicory)

100g (3½oz) Roquefort cheese, crumbled

dressing

1¼ tsp white-wine vinegar

½ tsp Dijon mustard

salt and pepper

½ tsp caster sugar, or to taste

2 tbsp walnut oil

1½ tbsp light olive oil

I Make the dressing by mixing all the ingredients, except the oils, together. Slowly whisk in the oils and then check the seasoning.

2 Cut the pears into slices lengthwise. If you are not serving immediately, squeeze fresh lemon juice over them to prevent browning. Just before serving, toss all the ingredients together with the dressing.

In *ceviche*, a speciality of South America, the lime juice 'cooks' the raw fish. Healthy as well as delicious.

· · · · · ·

salmon ceviche with avocado and mango

serves 4 as a main course

800g (1¾lb) salmon fillet, skin removed

juice of 2 limes

2 medium red chillies, deseeded and cut into slivers

2 spring onions, finely sliced

salt and pepper

1 mango (not so ripe that it's soft)

2 avocados

30g (1¼oz) coriander leaves and stalks

10g (¼oz) mint leaves

dressing

juice of 1 lime

5 tbsp olive oil

salt and pepper

1 tsp caster sugar, or to taste

I Cut the salmon into slices, about 2mm (⅟₁₆in) thick. Lay on a large plate or tray and squeeze the lime juice over the top. Scatter with the chilli and spring onion, and season well. Turn the pieces over so that everything gets coated and leave for 5 minutes.

2 Make a dressing by mixing the lime juice with the olive oil, some salt and pepper and the sugar. Taste to check whether you need to make any adjustments.

3 Peel the mango and cut off the 'cheeks': the fleshy parts on either side of the stone. Cut these cheeks into slices about the thickness of a 50-pence piece. (Use the rest of the mango flesh for something else; it is difficult to remove it and keep it firm and intact.) Halve the avocados and remove the stones. Cut each half into slices, then peel the skin from each slice. Work carefully to avoid squashing the flesh. Gently toss the mango and avocado with the herbs and the salmon. Serve at once.

Scandinavian-inspired. The cold acidity of the buttermilk really cuts through the richness of the bacon and fish. You can use smoked trout or fresh salmon instead of hot-smoked salmon, and can include quarters of cooked beetroot as well (but not pickled beetroot).

· · · · · ·

hot-smoked salmon, bacon and potato salad with buttermilk dressing

serves 4 as a main course

500g (18oz) small waxy potatoes

15g (½oz) butter

200g (7oz) green beans, topped

250g (9oz) pancetta or bacon lardons

400g (14oz) hot-smoked salmon

300g (10½oz) watercress

dressing

375ml (13fl oz) buttermilk

6 tbsp whipping cream

1 garlic clove, finely chopped

2 tbsp finely chopped dill

black pepper

I To make the dressing, mix everything together and put it in the refrigerator until you need it.

2 Try to cook everything (except the hot-smoked salmon, of course) at the last minute so that you have a salad which contains different temperatures.

3 Boil the potatoes until tender, drain and toss in the butter. Cover. Boil the beans until *al dente* and fry the bacon in its own fat until cooked and coloured on all sides.

4 Break up the salmon into very large flakes, discarding the skin. Gently toss the potatoes, watercress and beans with most of the buttermilk dressing, then put the salmon and bacon on top and drizzle over the rest of the dressing.

and also...

...smoked mackerel, potato and beetroot salad

Make the salad as above but use smoked mackerel instead of salmon (again, remove the skin), omit the bacon and use 200g (7oz) cooked beetroot. Halve or quarter the globes of beetroot and quickly sauté them in a little butter until they are warm. Arrange them with the rest of the salad at the last minute (otherwise the colour from the beetroot will stain the other ingredients) and dress.

Preserved or pickled lemons are now available in many supermarkets – a company called Belazu makes them.
You can serve this salad at room temperature rather than warm (which makes it a great lunch), but don't add the herbs until just before serving.

• • • • • •

warm chicken, roast pepper, chickpea and preserved lemon salad

serves 4

3 red peppers, halved, with stalk and seeds removed

olive oil

salt and pepper

4 chicken breast fillets, skinned

1 x 410g (14½oz) can chickpeas, drained and rinsed

1 preserved lemon, flesh discarded and skin cut into slivers

a good handful of flat-leaf parsley or coriander leaves (about 25g/1oz), very coarsely chopped

dressing

3 garlic cloves

40g (1½oz) pine nuts

85ml (3fl oz) extra-virgin olive oil

juice of ½ lemon

I Lay the peppers in a roasting tin. Drizzle over about 5 tbsp olive oil and season. Roast in an oven preheated to 190ºC/375ºF/gas mark 5 for about 35 minutes, or until the peppers are soft and slightly charred.

2 For the dressing, put the garlic and pine nuts into a food processor and, with the motor running, pour in the oil. Add the lemon juice and season to taste.

3 When the peppers are cooked, cut them into broad strips. You can remove the skin first but I hardly ever do.

4 Brush the chicken breasts with olive oil and season. Heat a ridged griddle pan and cook the breasts for about 2 minutes on each side; don't try to turn them before they have cooked for that long or you could tear the flesh. (Or you can simply fry the breasts in a frying pan.) Lower the heat and cook for another 2½-3 minutes on each side, or until the chicken is cooked through.

5 Slice the breasts and toss them with the chickpeas, roast pepper, preserved lemon, herbs and dressing. Serve immediately.

An utterly beautiful-looking winter salad. Who says cold-weather food has to be brown? I sometimes add torn mozzarella, crumbled goat cheese or Gorgonzola as well.

. . . . . .

pear, fig and prosciutto salad with pomegranates

serves 4

½ pomegranate

2 heads white chicory

2 heads red chicory

4 small pears

juice of 1 lemon

6 ripe figs, quartered

6 tbsp extra-virgin olive oil

salt and pepper

12 slices prosciutto

I To remove the seeds from the pomegranate, hold the half fruit over a bowl and beat hard with a wooden spoon; the seeds should tumble out. If they don't (your pomegranate may not be ripe enough), then gouge out the seeds with a spoon and remove the creamy, bitter pith attached to them. Pull the leaves of the chicories apart.

2 Halve and core the pears and cut into slices about 5mm (¼in) wide. Immediately put them into half the lemon juice and turn them over in it – this stops the flesh from turning brown.

3 Arrange the fig quarters, pear slices and chicory leaves on a platter. Drizzle some extra-virgin olive oil and pour the rest of the lemon juice over the top, and season. Tear the prosciutto into broad strips and lay these over the fruit and leaves. Scatter on the pomegranate seeds. Drizzle again with a little extra-virgin olive oil and scatter with some freshly ground black pepper. Serve immediately.

If you can't find Cashel Blue – a gorgeous Irish cheese which I always think tastes faintly of smoked bacon – then use Gorgonzola instead.

. . . . . .

salad of seared beef and cashel blue cheese

serves 4 as a starter

1 x 350g (12oz) piece fillet of beef, trimmed

salt and pepper

2 tbsp groundnut oil

85g (3oz) strongly flavoured leaves (such as rocket and watercress)

½ red onion, very finely sliced

125g (4½oz) Cashel Blue cheese, crumbled

dressing

¾ tbsp white-wine vinegar

a smidgen of Dijon mustard

a pinch of caster sugar

6 tbsp extra-virgin olive oil

I Make the dressing by whisking all the ingredients together with a fork.

2 Sprinkle the piece of beef with black pepper and salt. Heat the oil in a frying pan until very hot, then cook the fillet for about 2 minutes each side – the beef should remain totally rare inside. Leave the meat to rest a little.

3 Mix the salad leaves in a bowl with the onion and cheese and most of the dressing. Toss and divide among four plates. Slice the beef and lay it on top of the salads. Grind some pepper over the top and drizzle on the rest of the dressing.

The starter is my favourite part of any meal. It's small, designed to stimulate rather than sate the appetite, and can just be an assembly of good ingredients. For suppers with friends – especially mid-week – or when you just want to spoil yourself a bit, try the following. Evidence that simple can be very chic.

• • • • • •

(virtually) no-cook starters

radishes, sweet butter and sea salt
One of the chic-est starters imaginable. Get really fresh French breakfast radishes (the leaves should be sprightly, not droopy) and wash well. Serve with really good unsalted butter and a baguette or sourdough bread. The idea is to spread the peppery radishes with the butter and eat them with the salt and bread. Wrinkled black olives and rounds of salami are good along with this.

claqueret
One of those dishes you find in provincial French cheese shops or old-fashioned French homes. It's a light, slightly tangy dip, which you can spread on toasted *croûtes* (crostini) or serve with radishes. Simply mash together 300g (10½oz) mild goat cheese, 6 tbsp crème fraîche, 1 tbsp each of white-wine vinegar and dry white wine, 2 tbsp extra-virgin olive oil, 2 crushed garlic cloves, 2 tbsp each of chopped parsley and chives, and a good grinding of black pepper. Cover and refrigerate until you need it. It's best made the day before.

quail eggs with *dukkah*
A North African street snack, and a classy opener to a meal. Toast 55g (2oz) blanched hazelnuts in a dry frying pan, then toast 55g (2oz) sesame seeds with 3 tbsp each of cumin and coriander seeds. Let everything cool, then either pound the nuts and spices with a pestle and mortar, or pulse-blend them in a food processor (you want to end up with a powdery mixture, with coarse bits throughout, not a paste, so be careful if you are using a food processor). Cook the quail eggs in a pan of boiling water for 4 minutes and serve with sea salt and a bowl of *dukkah*.

eggs with mayo
Yes, hard-boiled eggs can be smart. Be sure to use a good bought mayo. Mix it with a couple of tbsp of fromage frais or crème fraîche and a good squeeze of lemon juice, and flavour with chopped black olives and anchovies, or shredded sorrel or other herbs such as chervil, basil or parsley, or finely chopped red onion and capers. Serve with hard-boiled hen eggs or quail eggs. Quail eggs take just 4 minutes to hard-boil.

spanish tapas
Tapas doesn't have to mean making tortillas or frying prawns. Just serve good, coarse country bread with rounds of *chorizo*, cured anchovies in olive oil (go for a really good brand such as Ortíz), *manchego* cheese and the quince jelly called *membrillo* (now available in many delis), Serrano ham or *jamón iberico* (the latter is an expensive but delicious cured ham, from pigs fed on acorns), with caperberries, salted almonds and green olives.

little potatoes with crème fraîche and *keta*

This became almost a cliché (totally *passé* as a smart canapé) but, as with many things that get labelled as 'so over', it is delicious and beautifully simple. Cook little waxy potatoes (La Ratte, Charlotte or Pink Fir are the varieties to look for, or Jersey Royals when they're in season) until tender, then serve them with a small bowl of *keta* (salmon caviar) and another bowl of crème fraîche and let guests help themselves.

asparagus

Still such a fleeting seasonal pleasure that it doesn't require much adornment. Serve steamed with melted butter, or with a couple of tubs of potted shrimps, which you've quickly heated and mixed with chopped dill (spoon the shrimps and butter on top of the asparagus). Or drizzle with extra-virgin olive oil, a touch of balsamic vinegar and shower with shavings of Parmesan.

prosciutto and fruit

Cured ham with fruit may take you back to the Italian *trattorias* which were edged out by more fashionable Italian peasant food, but it's still a great combination. Serve fatty pink slices with fresh figs, sliced ripe pears (prepare just before serving and squeeze a little lemon juice on the slices to stop them going brown), or peeled wedges of mango.

broad beans, ham and pecorino

This makes a lovely starter when the beans first come into season in May, when they are small and sweet enough to eat raw. Just remove the beans from the pod and toss them with shavings of pecorino cheese, slivers of prosciutto, black pepper and extra-virgin olive oil. You can blanch the broad beans if you prefer, then slip off their little thin skins, to reveal a wonderful, bright greenness, before combining with the other ingredients.

vegetables in *pinzimonio*

Simple and very summery. Provide each diner with a little glass or bowl full of really good extra-virgin olive oil (about 75ml/2½fl oz per person; it is worth splashing out on a delicious single-estate oil). Have sea salt and black pepper available. Serve with a platter of perfect raw vegetables, or a mixture of raw and blanched vegetables. Cherry tomatoes, thin slices of fennel, florets of cauliflower, young carrots, blanched green beans, steamed asparagus, cooked artichoke heart – whatever is good and in season.

vegetables with *bagna cauda*

A Piedmontese dish, though there's also a Provençal version. Serve perfect raw or cooked vegetables (or a mixture of raw and cooked – I often include strips of roast pepper) with an anchovy dipping sauce. Gently heat 200ml (7fl oz) olive oil with 40g (1½oz) butter and add 2 garlic cloves, peeled and very finely chopped. Cook until soft but not coloured, then add 10 chopped anchovy fillets and cook until the anchovies have disintegrated. Add pepper. That's it. Ideally this should be kept warm with a little burner underneath it, but it does retain its heat for a while so just serve one bowl or individual little ramekins of it. Hard-boiled hen or quail eggs are good with this, too.

rye bread and hot-smoked salmon

A bit different from brown bread and cold-smoked salmon. Butter squares or triangles of rye bread and top with pieces of hot-smoked salmon (remove the skin), a tsp of sour cream and a sprig of dill.

toast *skagen*

Swedish and very easy to throw together. Combine 450g (1lb) peeled prawns with 125ml (4fl oz) sour cream, 125ml (4fl oz) mayonnaise, lemon juice and plenty of chopped dill and chives. Toast rounds of bread and top with the prawn mixture and a little *keta* (salmon eggs), if you can run to the expense.

(virtually) no-cook starters

I love aubergines. They look like Ali Baba's slippers and have a velvety flesh that will absorb a whole array of flavours but still taste of itself. I'm not so fond of frying or grilling them as it takes an age, but have found that slices can be roasted successfully as long as they are well coated in oil.

And don't get in a tizz about the amount of oil; it is olive, after all. All of these make good starters or side dishes, or are good as part of a spread of Mediterranean *mezze* or *antipasti*.

· · · · · ·

roast aubergine three ways

serves 4 as a starter or side dish

3 aubergines

olive oil

salt and pepper

lemon juice or balsamic vinegar (optional)

I Trim the ends off the aubergines and cut them lengthwise into slices about 8mm (⅜in) thick. Toss the slices in a bowl (you can do this in batches) with olive oil, salt and pepper. Use your hands to make sure they are covered and that the oil is rubbed in. Put them on metal baking sheets and roast for about 25 minutes in an oven preheated to 200°C/400°F/gas mark mark 6. The aubergines should be golden and soft. If they're at all dry leave them to marinate in lemon juice (or a little balsamic vinegar) and extra-virgin olive oil. Try serving them...

...with pecorino and chilli

Halve 2 red chillies, deseed and cut into fine strips. Gently sauté with 4 finely sliced garlic cloves until pale gold and scatter over the aubergine. Squeeze the juice of ½ lemon on top, season, shower with shavings of pecorino (use a potato peeler) and drizzle with extra-virgin olive oil.

...with hummus, yogurt, mint and coriander

Whiz a 410g (14½oz) can chickpeas (drained), 150ml (5fl oz) extra-virgin olive oil, the juice of 1 lemon, 1 garlic clove, 1½ tbsp tahini, 1 heaped tsp cayenne pepper and 1 tsp ground cumin in a food processor. Season. Tear mint and coriander leaves over the aubergine slices and serve with the hummus with plain Greek yogurt spooned alongside.

...with *salsa verde*

Into a food processor put 8 anchovy fillets, 10 basil leaves, 15 mint leaves, a small bunch of flat-leaf parsley (leaves only), ½ tbsp Dijon mustard, 1 garlic clove and 1 tbsp capers, rinsed of salt or brine. Pulse-mix, adding 150ml (5fl oz) extra-virgin olive oil. Taste and add lemon juice. Serve spooned over the aubergine slices.

serves 4 as a starter or side dish

4 aubergines

olive oil

salt and pepper

2 onions, finely sliced

6 garlic cloves, finely sliced

2 medium red chillies, halved, deseeded and finely sliced

juice of ½ lemon

100g (3½oz) feta cheese, crumbled

200g (7oz) Greek yogurt

a handful of mint leaves, torn

extra-virgin olive oil

I've never eaten this in Turkey. Somebody described it to me, and I came up with this dish – so I can't claim it as authentic but who cares? It is a lip-smacking combination of textures and temperatures. Substantial enough to be a main course if you want to serve it that way.

· · · · · ·

turkish baked aubergines with chilli, feta and mint

I Halve the aubergines lengthwise and then score a trellis pattern into the flesh of each half on the cut surface, being careful not to cut all the way through. Pour about 10 tbsp of olive oil over them and season. Turn them over to make sure they are well coated. Put into an oven preheated to 200ºC/400ºF/gas mark 6 and roast for 40-45 minutes.

2 While the aubergines are cooking, sauté the onions in 4 tbsp olive oil until soft and golden. Add the garlic and chilli and cook for another 2 minutes, until they are soft as well.

3 When the aubergines are tender put them on a serving plate, cut-side up, and squeeze lemon juice over them. Gently press the cooked flesh down to make a bit of room for the onions. Fill the aubergine cavities with the onion-and-chilli mix and scatter the feta on top.

4 Daub the yogurt over the aubergines and throw on the mint leaves. Drizzle some extra-virgin olive oil over the top before serving. You can serve this warm or at room temperature.

Summer arrives and you can find yourself serving nothing but bowls of claggy potato salad. Dress potatoes while they're still hot, leave them so that the waxy flesh can soak up the flavours, and you have quite a different dish. You can eat this warm or at room temperature, and make it well ahead of when you want to serve it.

Use little waxy potatoes such as Pink Fir Apple, La Ratte or Charlotte for these recipes.

· · · · · ·

warm potatoes and beans with avocado

and also...

...warm potatoes and beans with pesto

Prepare the potatoes and beans as below, using 400g/14oz potatoes and 150g/5½oz green beans. While they are cooking, make some pesto by whizzing 45g (1½oz) freshly grated Parmesan, 1 garlic clove, 45g (1½oz) pine nuts, 55g (2oz) basil leaves and 85ml (3fl oz) extra-virgin olive oil in a food processor. Taste and season. Toss the cooked vegetables with a couple of tbsp extra-virgin olive oil and season. Add a little of the bean cooking water to the pesto to loosen it, then toss the pesto with the vegetables. Great with lamb.

...potatoes with shallots and capers

Cook 600g (1lb 5oz) potatoes as in the main recipe. Slice 4 shallots and cook them in 1 tbsp olive oil until they are soft but not coloured. Put these in a serving bowl with 1½ tbsp rinsed capers and about 1 tbsp chopped flat-leaf parsley. As soon as the potatoes are tender, drain them and add them to the bowl with 2 tbsp extra-virgin olive oil, ½ tbsp white-wine vinegar, salt and pepper. Toss everything gently together and serve hot, warm or at room temperature. This is especially good with fish.

serves 4 as a side dish

1 avocado

300g (10½oz) small waxy potatoes

100g (3½oz) green beans, topped but not tailed

dressing

¾ tbsp white-wine vinegar

a drop of Dijon mustard

salt and pepper

a good pinch of caster sugar

5½ tbsp extra-virgin olive oil

1 Make the dressing by whisking all the ingredients together with a fork.

2 Halve the avocado and remove the stone. Without peeling the avocado, cut each half lengthwise into slices about 8mm (⅜in) thick at the thickest part. Peel the skin from each slice and place the slices in the bottom of a shallow serving bowl. Pour the dressing over.

3 Cook the potatoes in boiling salted water, for 10-15 minutes, depending on how small they are, until just tender. Cook the beans while the potatoes are boiling (they should still have a little firmness) then drain and run cold water over them to keep the bright-green colour. Put the beans in the bowl with the avocado. Slice each potato in half, add to the bowl and gently toss everything together. Using your hands is the easiest way – you just have to be careful not to break up the avocado. Serve immediately, while the potatoes are still warm.

Potatoes crushed with olive oil are a bit of a cliché of modern restaurant menus, but that doesn't mean they're not good. These are great with grilled or baked fish on top.

· · · · · ·

potatoes with olives and lemon

serves 4 as a side dish

800g (1¾lb) new potatoes, scrubbed

175g (6oz) black olives in olive oil, stoned

8 tbsp extra-virgin olive oil, plus extra for drizzling

juice of ½ lemon

finely grated rind of 1 lemon

2 tbsp coarsely chopped flat-leaf parsley

salt and pepper

I Cook the potatoes in boiling salted water until tender. Drain but keep the potatoes in the saucepan so they stay warm while you add the other ingredients. Partly crush the potatoes with a masher or fork – you just want them broken up, not mashed – and stir through the rest of the ingredients. Season, drizzle with a little olive oil and serve.

Kind of Spanish, I suppose (it's that smoked paprika again). Good with roast or grilled chicken or lamb or highly spiced sausages. Topped with a fried egg, it makes a pretty good supper dish.

· · · · · ·

roast potatoes and tomatoes with spices

serves 6 as a side dish

1kg (2¼lb) waxy potatoes, cut into even-sized pieces

500g (18oz) cherry tomatoes, left whole

1 tbsp coriander seeds and 1½ tsp cumin seeds

2 tsp smoked paprika (*Pimentón de la Vera*)

6 tbsp olive oil

salt and pepper

4 tbsp finely chopped parsley or coriander leaves

I Spread out the potatoes and tomatoes in a single layer in a roasting tin.

2 In a small frying pan, dry-roast the coriander and cumin seeds. Crush them in a mortar, and add the smoked paprika and olive oil. Pour over the vegetables, making sure they all get coated, and season well with salt and pepper. Roast in an oven preheated to 180ºC/350ºF/gas mark 4 for 40 minutes, shaking the tin a couple of times during cooking. Scatter with chopped herbs and serve at once.

Roast tomatoes are a cinch, and roasting is a good way to treat those that are lacking in flavour as it concentrates the sugar content. Make sure you lay the tomatoes in a single layer so that they really roast and don't just sweat.

• • • • • •

roast tomatoes with herbs and lemon crumbs

serves 6 as a side dish

12 plum tomatoes

4 tbsp olive oil

salt and pepper

a little caster sugar

30g (1¼oz) fresh white breadcrumbs

finely grated zest of ½ lemon

¼ tbsp finely chopped parsley

¼ tbsp chopped chives

and also...

...roast tomatoes with goat cheese

Make as below, but instead of sprinkling with breadcrumbs, top the tomatoes with 125g (4½oz) crumbled goat cheese. Drizzle with a little more olive oil, grind on some black pepper and bake for another 10 minutes, until the cheese is starting to turn pale gold.

...hot and sweet roast tomatoes

Prepare the tomatoes as below. Mix 4 tbsp olive oil, 2 tbsp balsamic vinegar, 1 tsp *harissa* and 1 tsp caster sugar in a cup. Pour this over the tomatoes and roast for 45 minutes at 200°C/400°F/gas mark 6. The tomatoes should be shrunken and sweet. Serve warm or at room temperature, drizzled with extra-virgin olive oil and either daubed with plain yogurt or scattered with black olives and torn basil leaves.

...baked tomatoes with parmesan

Follow the main roast tomato recipe. Throw about 55g (2oz) grated Parmesan over the tomato halves about 15 minutes before the end of cooking. For a creamy cheese gratin, pour 150ml (5fl oz) double cream over the tomatoes at the end of the cooking time, sprinkle with the cheese, and bake for another 15 minutes until the cheese is bubbling and golden.

I Cut each tomato in half and spread in a single layer in a large *gratin* dish or roasting tin. Drizzle with about half of the olive oil, and season. Using your hands, mix the tomatoes around so that they are well covered with oil. Turn them all cut-side up. Put into an oven preheated to 190°C/375°F/gas mark 5 and roast for 40 minutes, sprinkling a little sugar over the top after they have cooked for 20 minutes.

2 Take the tomatoes out and sprinkle on the breadcrumbs, lemon zest and herbs. Drizzle again with olive oil and put back in the oven for another 15 minutes, or until the breadcrumbs are golden. Serve hot or warm.

A spin on roast Mediterranean vegetables, and very easy to make. Serve as a main course with flatbread or a bowl of couscous into which you have stirred some chopped parsley and maybe some slivers of preserved lemon. It's also a good side dish with roast or grilled chicken or lamb.

· · · · · ·

hot and sweet roast mediterranean vegetables with tahini dressing

serves 4 as main course, 6 as a side dish

3 courgettes

2 aubergines

1 red pepper and 1 yellow pepper

6 tomatoes

1 red onion

4 tbsp olive oil

1 tbsp balsamic vinegar

3 tsp ground cumin

½ tsp ground cinnamon

2 tsp soft dark brown sugar

2 tsp *harissa* or West Indian hot sauce

salt and pepper

55g (2oz) raisins

45g (1½oz) pine nuts, toasted

2 tbsp roughly chopped coriander leaves

dressing

150g (5½oz) plain yogurt

150g (5½oz) tahini

juice of 2 lemons

4 tbsp water

4 tbsp extra-virgin olive oil

4 garlic cloves, crushed

salt and pepper

I Cut the courgettes and the aubergine into rounds about 1cm (½in) thick. Cut the larger aubergine slices in quarters and halve the rest. Halve and deseed the peppers and cut each half into 4 or 5 broad strips lengthwise. Quarter the tomatoes and cut the onion into half-moon-shaped slices.

2 Put the vegetables into a large roasting tin in a single layer. Mix the oil, vinegar, cumin, cinnamon, sugar and *harissa* or hot sauce together. Pour this over the vegetables and season well with salt and pepper. Stir the vegetables round to make sure they are all coated. Roast in an oven preheated to 190ºC/375ºF/gas mark 5 for 25 minutes.

3 Put the raisins in just-boiled water and leave to soak for 20 minutes, then drain and stir into the vegetables. Roast for another 15 minutes or so, or until the vegetables are tender and slightly charred. Stir in the pine nuts.

4 To make the dressing, beat the yogurt into the tahini with a fork or spoon, then add the lemon juice, water, olive oil and garlic. Taste and season with salt and pepper – it needs quite a lot of salt. You may also want to add a little more water or olive oil to thin the mixture.

5 Put the vegetables on a large platter. Leave at room temperature if you are serving in a couple of hours' time, or refrigerate and bring back to room temperature before you want to serve them. Drizzle with the dressing, scatter the coriander over the top and serve.

and also…

…roast mediterranean vegetables with pickled lemons
Roast the vegetables as in the main recipe but omit the sugar, spices, raisins, pine nuts and coriander. About 10 minutes before the vegetables are due to be ready, stir in the sliced rind of ¾ preserved lemon. The sweetness of the vegetables and sourness of the lemon are delicious together.

…roast mediterranean vegetables with anchovy pesto
Roast the vegetables as in the main recipe but omit the sugar, spices, raisins, pine nuts and coriander. Put a 50g (1¾oz) can anchovies in oil, 70g (2½oz) pine nuts and 1 garlic clove in a food processor. Turn it on and add 100ml (3½fl oz) extra-virgin olive oil in a steady stream. Taste and add as much lemon juice as you think it needs (I generally end up adding a little less than ½ lemon), season with pepper and stir in a small bunch of chopped flat-leaf parsley. Serve drizzled over the vegetables. This sauce is also good with roasted red peppers.

…roast mediterranean vegetables with white bean *skordalia*
Skordalia is a Greek garlic sauce, usually made with potato, nuts or bread. This is a bean one. It's good as a dip for raw vegetables, too, and as an accompaniment to grilled fish or lamb. Be sure to pay attention to the seasoning – you need to be generous. Roast the vegetables as in the main recipe but omit the sugar, spices, raisins, pine nuts and coriander. Heat 2 tbsp olive oil in a saucepan and cook ½ chopped onion until soft. Add 5 chopped garlic cloves and cook for another couple of minutes, then purée these with a drained 410g (14½oz) can of cannellini beans, 100ml (3½fl oz) extra-virgin olive oil, the juice of ½ lemon and plenty of salt and pepper. Check seasoning. Serve at room temperature with the roast vegetables.

This may sound like a simple and not very exciting combination, but I practically live on it in the summer when my small patch of courgettes produces more vegetables than I can cope with. It's also well behaved – you can make it earlier in the day to eat in the evening

• • • • • •

courgettes with ricotta, mint and basil

serves 4 as a main course, 6 as a side dish

6 medium courgettes

olive oil

salt and pepper

375g (13oz) ricotta cheese, fresh if possible, broken into chunks

40g (1½oz) pecorino cheese shavings

1 small bunch basil, leaves only

1 small bunch mint, leaves only

juice of 1 lemon

extra-virgin olive oil

1 Have everything ready and to hand as you will layer the dish as you cook it.

2 Cut the courgettes into rounds about 5mm (¼in) thick. Heat 2 tbsp olive oil in a large pan and cook the courgettes, in batches, until golden on each side and tender. Add more olive oil as you need it and season the courgettes as you cook them. Put the courgettes in the bottom of a broad shallow bowl and cook the next batch. When you have a layer, then put some ricotta, pecorino and herbs on the top, plus a good squeeze of lemon and a drizzle of extra-virgin olive oil. Continue like this until you've layered all the courgettes. Finish with some herbs and shavings of pecorino and drizzle with a bit of extra-virgin olive oil. Serve while still warm, or at room temperature.

One of the easiest and best-liked dishes I cook. You can use this stuffing as a kind of blueprint and add a little chopped red chilli and anchovies, or some sautéed spicy sausage and onion.

• • • • • •

sicilian baked stuffed peppers

serves 6 as a starter or a side dish

150g (5½oz) fresh white breadcrumbs from a coarse country bread with a good flavour

55g (2oz) currants

75g (2¾oz) pine nuts, toasted

45g (1½oz) capers, rinsed of salt or brine

45g (1½oz) black olives, pitted and chopped

15g (½oz) combined parsley and mint leaves, roughly chopped

4 tbsp olive oil, plus extra for drizzling

salt and pepper

6 large red peppers, halved and deseeded

I Mix all the ingredients together, except the peppers. Taste; even though the stuffing is still raw, you've got to get an idea of how much salt to add, if any.

2 Put the pepper halves into an ovenproof dish and spoon the stuffing into them. Drizzle some more olive oil over the top and bake in an oven preheated to 180°C/350°F/gas mark 4 for 1 hour. Serve hot or leave to cool to room temperature.

and also...

...roast peppers with tomatoes, mozzarella and basil
Halve and deseed 6 red peppers, then put ½ garlic clove, finely sliced, and 2-3 cherry tomatoes in each half. Drizzle with olive oil, season and roast in an oven preheated to 180°C/350°F/gas mark 4 for 40 minutes. Put a thick slice of mozzarella on top of each pepper half, drizzle with more oil and put back in the oven for 10 minutes until the mozzarella has melted. Serve each pepper half topped with a slug of extra-virgin olive oil, freshly ground black pepper and basil leaves.

You can make this with tender-stem broccoli or ordinary broccoli, as the season for purple-sprouting is, sadly, so short. With its little leaves and mauve heads, many people like purple-sprouting broccoli just as much as asparagus, and you can treat it in similar ways. Eat it with melted butter or dip it into a soft-boiled egg.

A salad of warm purple-sprouting broccoli drizzled with a little balsamic vinegar, extra-virgin olive oil and topped with shavings of Parmesan and a poached egg is also delicious. Broccoli stands up well to strong flavours such as chilli and anchovy. If you don't want to cook it with anchovies, as in the second recipe, steam and then toss with vinaigrette into which you have snipped some cured anchovies.

• • • • • •

purple-sprouting broccoli with chilli and garlic

serves 4 as a side dish

300g (10½oz) purple-sprouting broccoli

5 tbsp olive oil

4 garlic cloves, finely sliced

¾ tsp dried chilli flakes

salt and pepper

75ml (2½fl oz) dry vermouth or dry white wine

extra-virgin olive oil, to drizzle (optional)

I Snip the rough ends off the broccoli and cut the larger pieces in half lengthwise. Remove any little leaves that don't look spanking fresh.

2 Heat the olive oil in a frying pan or sauté pan and add the broccoli. Stir-fry for about 3 minutes, on a high heat first of all, and then turn down to medium; it's just nice to get a little searing on the broccoli. Add the garlic and chilli flakes and cook until the garlic is pale gold. Season and add the vermouth or wine. Let the vermouth bubble a little, then cover with a lid and let the broccoli finish cooking in the steam created by the vermouth. Cook until just tender – about 4 minutes, but it does depend on the thickness of your broccoli, so check by piercing a stem with a sharp knife. Serve drizzled with a little extra-virgin olive oil if you like.

and also…

…purple-sprouting broccoli with anchovy cream

Cook the broccoli as above but, just before you add the vermouth, push the broccoli to one side of the pan and add 8 anchovy fillets. Cook the anchovies, mashing them with your spoon, until they've started to disintegrate. Pour on some dry white wine – about 75ml (2½fl oz) – and finish as above.

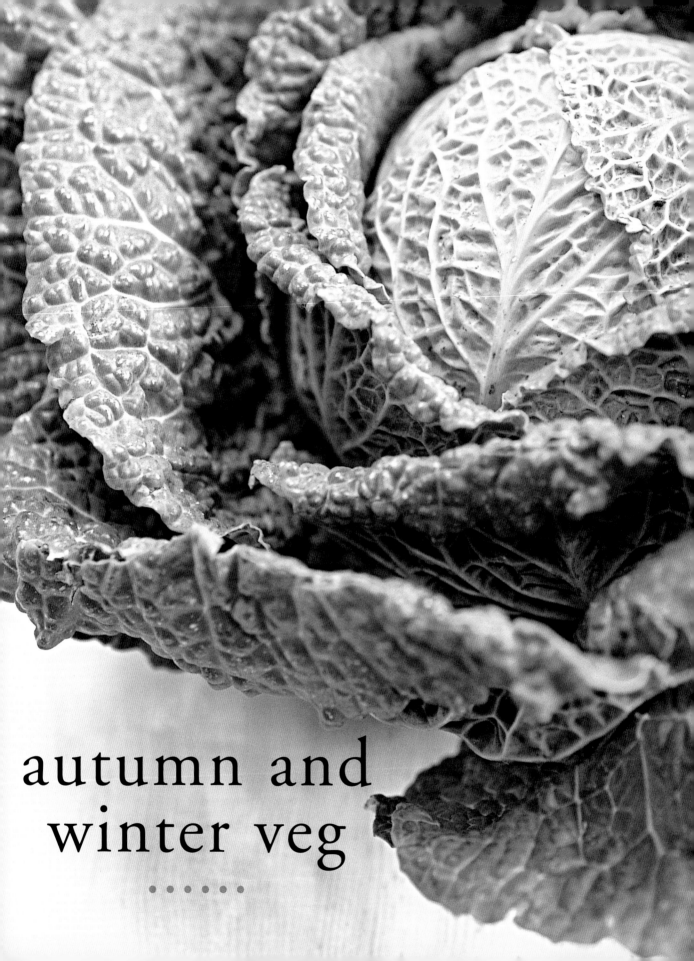

autumn and
winter veg

Most recipes for roast parsnips call for them to be parboiled before being roasted. I can rarely be bothered so I roast them from raw, but it does mean that you need to use parsnips that aren't too old and woody.

· · · · · ·

ginger, orange and honey roast parsnips

serves 4 as a side dish

400g (14oz) parsnips

1 large onion

25g (1oz) unsalted butter

juice of ½ orange

8 big tbsp runny honey

2 tsp ground ginger

leaves from 4 sprigs thyme

salt and pepper

1 Trim the parsnips. Halve them and quarter the larger ones. Halve the onion and cut each piece into half-moon-shaped slices, about 1cm (½in) thick at the thickest part.

2 Put the parsnips and onion into an ovenproof dish or roasting tin, and dot with little chunks of butter. Mix the orange juice with the honey and ginger. Pour two-thirds of this over the vegetables, add the thyme and season well with salt and pepper.

3 Put into an oven preheated to 180°C/350°F/gas mark mark 4. Cook for 30 minutes, then pour over the rest of the orange juice mix and put back in the oven. Cook for another 20–30 minutes. The parsnips should be soft, with caramelized tips, and the juice should have been absorbed. Serve immediately.

We don't make enough of beetroot, unlike the Scandinavians who pair its warm sweetness with the saltiness of smoked fish. This is lovely with boiled little waxy potatoes and fillets of hot smoked trout or salmon, or with baked fresh salmon.

· · · · · ·

swedish baked beetroot with onions, sour cream and dill

serves 4-6 as a side dish

750g (1lb 10oz) raw beetroot (try to get small ones)

4 tbsp olive oil

salt and pepper

2 red onions, cut into half-moon-shaped wedges

150ml (5fl oz) sour cream

1 tbsp roughly chopped dill

I Wrap the unpeeled beetroot in a foil parcel, drizzle with half the olive oil, season and put in a roasting tin. Cook in an oven preheated to 180ºC/350ºF/gas mark 4 until tender. (How long this takes depends on the size of your beetroot – it could take as long as 1½ hours.) Put the onion wedges in a small roasting tin, drizzle with the rest of the olive oil, season and roast in the same oven for 20-30 minutes. The onions should be tender and slightly singed at the tips.

2 When the beetroot is tender, peel each one (or leave the skin on if you prefer) and quarter or halve, depending on their size. Season the beetroot and put on a serving dish with the onions. Daub the sour cream over the vegetables and sprinkle with the dill. Serve hot or at room temperature.

potatoes without end...

If you're tired or short of time, tossing a green salad is the minimum amount of effort you need to make to ensure you get your veg fix, but we love carbs and they always take a bit more time. I roast potatoes drizzled with olive oil, or bake them in a whole host of ways. Potatoes are brilliant at absorbing different flavours, and I never stop feeling delighted that you put something as basic as spuds in the oven and, 30 minutes later, take out a lovely, golden dishful of food. You have to use a roasting tin or ovenproof dish in which your potatoes can lie in a single layer. I use a metal roasting tin or a cast-iron Le Creuset *gratin* dish as they both conduct heat well.

rosemary, garlic and olive oil roast potatoes

serves 4

675g (1½lb) small baby potatoes, cut into chunks about the size of a walnut

4 tbsp olive oil

1 tbsp balsamic vinegar

2 garlic bulbs, cloves separated, unpeeled

6 branches fresh rosemary, leaves of half removed from the stalks

salt and pepper

You can use either small new potatoes, or waxy varieties, such as Charlotte and Pink Fir Apple, or floury-textured potatoes such as King Edward's; they'll give you different but equally good results. Adapt the recipe by adding different spices – smoked paprika, dried chilli flakes or ground cumin and coriander – and omitting the rosemary. Add softer vegetables – chunks of aubergine, courgette or halved tomatoes – after the first 10 minutes' cooking time and toss them around in the oil, too.

• Mix all the ingredients together in a shallow ovenproof dish or roasting tin. The potatoes need to lie in a single layer. Cook for 35 minutes in an oven preheated to 200°C/400°F/gas mark 6, or until the potatoes are tender. Give the dish a good shake from time to time to make sure all the sides get a bit of browning.

balsamic roast potatoes and mushrooms

This is particularly good with grilled duck or steak.

serves 6

675g (1½lb) small waxy potatoes, halved

7 tbsp olive oil

3 tbsp balsamic vinegar

salt and pepper

about 6 branches thyme

8 large flat field mushrooms, cleaned and cut into thick slices

• Put the potatoes into a shallow ovenproof dish, leaving enough room for the mushrooms later. Pour over half the oil and balsamic, season and mix with your hands. Add the thyme and roast in an oven preheated to 200°C/400°F/gas mark 6 for 15 minutes. Add the mushrooms and the rest of the oil and vinegar, season again and stir everything around. It looks as if there are too many mushrooms, but they will shrink. Cook for another 15 minutes or so, stirring twice more, until the potatoes are tender and dark.

drunken potatoes

serves 6

900g (2lb) small waxy potatoes

100ml (3½fl oz) each of chicken stock and white wine

15g (½oz) butter

freshly ground black pepper

a small handful of finely chopped parsley

Another blueprint recipe, this one for baking potatoes in stock. Adapt it by using red wine and a couple of tbsp of olive oil instead of butter, and adding a few tsp of crushed coriander seeds and a bay leaf, and you have drunken potatoes, Greek style. I don't add salt to these as the reduced chicken stock provides enough.

• Halve the potatoes and put them in a roasting tin or ovenproof dish. Heat the stock and wine together with the butter until boiling and pour over the potatoes. Season. Cook in an oven preheated to 200°C/400°F/gas mark 6 for 45 minutes. You'll need to turn the potatoes over halfway through the cooking time. The liquid should have been completely absorbed by the end; cook for a little longer if it isn't. Sprinkle with the parsley and serve.

baked potatoes with chorizo

serves 6

900g (2lb) small waxy potatoes

3 onions

200ml (7fl oz) chicken stock

a good pinch of saffron strands

freshly ground black pepper

250g (9oz) *chorizo*, skin removed, cut into slices about 3mm (⅛in) thick

a small handful of finely chopped parsley or coriander

This is very good with meaty fish such as monkfish. The Spanish love *chorizo* and other pork products with fish. The combination works well.

• Halve the potatoes and put them in a shallow ovenproof dish or roasting tin. Halve the onions, cut each half into four wedges and add them, too. Heat the chicken stock with the saffron and, once it's boiling, pour it over the vegetables. Season. Put in an oven preheated to 200°C/400°F/gas mark 6 and cook for 45 minutes, stirring the vegetables around, and adding the *chorizo* halfway through the cooking time. The vegetables should be tender and the stock should have been absorbed by the end of the cooking time. If there is still liquid left, then cook a little longer. Scatter with the parsley or coriander and serve.

baked potatoes with orange

serves 6

900g (2lb) small waxy potatoes

4 onions

125ml (4fl oz) chicken stock

75ml (2½fl oz) orange juice

15g (½oz) butter

2 tbsp marmalade

10 juniper seeds, crushed

freshly ground black pepper

Great with roast lamb or duck, or grilled duck breast.

• Halve the potatoes and put them in a roasting tin or ovenproof dish. Halve the onions, cut each half into four wedges and add them, too. Heat the stock, orange juice, butter and marmalade together, helping the marmalade to melt by pressing it with the back of a spoon. Bring to the boil and pour over the potatoes. Scatter the juniper seeds over the top and season with pepper. Cook in an oven preheated to 200°C/400°F/gas mark 6 for 50-60 minutes, stirring the potatoes around halfway through the cooking time. When cooked, the potatoes should be tender and golden and the liquid absorbed.

autumn and winter veg

Good with warm or cold poached salmon in the spring and summer. This is also excellent with smoked sausages in the winter, especially if you stir in some caraway seeds (fried in a little butter first) instead of the dill.

• • • • • •

scandinavian potatoes in sour cream

serves 4-6

1kg (2¼lb) small, waxy potatoes

salt and pepper

6 tbsp hot chicken stock

6 tbsp sour cream

a couple of fronds of dill, chopped

a good squeeze of lemon

I Cook the potatoes in boiling salted water until just tender. There's no need to peel them unless you really want to.

2 Drain the potatoes, add all the other ingredients and mix gently, making sure that all the potatoes are nicely coated. Put into a warmed bowl and serve.

I wanted an easy accompaniment for Indian meat dishes. This seemed like the most hassle-free option and it's so good that I now serve the vegetables as a meal in their own right, with rice, chutneys and plain yogurt.

• • • • • •

roast vegetables with indian spices

serves 6

2 sweet potatoes, peeled and cut into large chunks

300g (10½oz) carrots, trimmed and halved lengthwise

1 butternut squash, peeled, deseeded and cut into long wedges

2 large onions, each one cut into 6 wedges

1 tbsp ground cumin

1½ tsp ground coriander

3 tsp chilli powder

1 tsp ground ginger

salt and pepper

6 tbsp sunflower oil

1 bunch coriander, leaves coarsely chopped

I Put everything except the fresh coriander in a single layer in a large roasting tin and mix together with your hands. Roast in an oven preheated to 190°C/375°F/gas mark 5 for 45 minutes or until tender, turning the vegetables every so often. Sprinkle on the coriander leaves before serving.

This is the kind of dish I usually hate as it mixes elements from completely different cuisines – a Thai-inspired dressing with Greek yogurt – but it works. It's such a satisfying mixture of hot, sour, salty and sweet, and a contrast of temperatures, too. Once you've eaten it, you'll crave it. The potatoes are good on their own with just a green salad, or as an accompaniment to roast or grilled chicken.

· · · · · ·

baked sweet potato with coriander and chilli relish

serves 4

4 sweet potatoes

200g (7oz) plain Greek yogurt

relish

40g (1½oz) fresh coriander

3 garlic cloves

juice of 1 lime

1 tsp caster sugar

2 tbsp olive oil

1 piece fresh root ginger, about 1cm (½in) square, peeled and grated

¼ tbsp fish sauce

1 medium red chilli, halved, deseeded and finely chopped

I You don't need to prepare the sweet potatoes in any way. Simply bake them in an oven preheated to 190ºC/375ºF/gas mark 5 for about 45 minutes, depending on size, until tender when pierced with a skewer.

2 While the potatoes are cooking. put all the ingredients for the relish (except for the chilli) in a blender and whiz.

3 Split the potatoes down the middle lengthwise, as you would a regular baked potato, and spoon some yogurt inside. Add the chilli to the relish, then spoon some of this on top of the yogurt and serve.

and also...

...baked sweet potato with goat cheese and olive and walnut relish

Bake the sweet potatoes as above and, while they're cooking, put 55g (2oz) walnut pieces, a garlic clove and a small handful of chopped flat-leaf parsley into a mortar and pound with a pestle, gradually adding 2 tbsp extra-virgin olive oil, until you have a coarse, thick paste. Add the chopped flesh of 175g (6oz) black olives and pound again, but don't beat the olives into a paste – they should still have some texture. Stir in a good squeeze of lemon juice and season. Split the sweet potatoes down the middle and divide 150g (5½oz) crumbled goat cheese among them. Spoon some of the walnut and olive relish on top.

This always looks so good – a big dish of golden and tawny vegetables with singed tips – and requires no care whatsoever. You can add chunks of sweet potato, slices of squash and halved small beetroot to the mixture, and flavour with rosemary or sage instead of thyme.

· · · · · ·

roast autumn vegetables

serves 6

750g (1lb 10oz) small waxy potatoes or larger floury potatoes

400g (14oz) carrots, trimmed and halved lengthwise if large

400g (14oz) parsnips, trimmed and halved lengthwise

3 red onions, each cut into 6 wedges

4 tbsp olive oil

1 tbsp balsamic vinegar

leaves from a couple of sprigs of thyme, plus 5 whole sprigs

salt and pepper

I Cut the potatoes into chunks about the size of a walnut, though some waxy varieties are very small and may not need to be cut. Put all the vegetables into a large roasting tin – they should be able to lie in a single layer – and add the olive oil, vinegar, thyme leaves and seasoning. Toss everything together with your hands.

2 Roast in an oven preheated to 190°C/375°F/gas mark 5 for 45–60 minutes, until the vegetables are tender. Give them a bit of a shake every so often and add the thyme sprigs halfway through cooking time. Cover the dish with foil if some of the vegetables are getting too dark, though it's good if some of them end up slightly charred at the tips.

and also...

...maple and mustard roast vegetables

Make as above and spoon 4 tbsp dark maple syrup mixed with 4 tbsp grain mustard evenly over the vegetables 10 minutes before the end of cooking time.

...roast jerusalem artichokes with onions, lemon and thyme

Take 450g (1lb) Jerusalem artichokes – cut off the more knobbly bits and wash well, but don't peel them – and halve the larger ones lengthwise. Put into a roasting tin with 2 onions, cut into wedges. Throw in 6 sprigs of thyme, the juice of 1 lemon and 5 tbsp olive oil. Season and toss around with your hands. Cook as above.

This is adapted from a recipe in Claudia Roden's fabulous *A Book of Middle Eastern Food*. I usually eat it with plain boiled rice or couscous and yogurt as an easy mid-week supper.

. . . . . .

middle eastern lentils and peppers

serves 4 as a main course

4 tbsp olive oil

1 large leek, washed and cut into rounds

1 red pepper, halved, deseeded and sliced

½ tbsp ground cumin and 2 tsp ground coriander

1 red chilli, deseeded and chopped (or chilli sauce)

200g (7oz) red lentils

300ml (10fl oz) water or stock (a stock cube is fine)

1 x 400g (14oz) can tomatoes in thick juice

1 tsp caster sugar

1 tbsp tomato purée

salt and pepper

a large handful of coriander leaves, coarsely chopped

I Heat the olive oil in a heavy-bottomed saucepan and add the leek and pepper. Cook for about 10 minutes, until soft. Stir in the spices and cook for 2 minutes, then add all the other ingredients except the fresh coriander and simmer over a gentle heat for about 25 minutes until the lentils have collapsed. Taste for seasoning and stir in the fresh coriander. Serve with plain yogurt or tzatziki (see page 49).

Poor onions: always in the chorus line, never the star. Well, not here. A dish for all those who fight over the one onion that roasts inside the chicken. (Isn't that everyone?)

. . . . . .

melting roast onions

serves 6 as a side dish

6 medium onions, about 150g (5½oz) each, skins on

4 tbsp olive oil

salt and pepper

55g (2oz) butter

I Trim the base of the onions without removing the root. Cut a deep cross from the top to three-quarters of the way down each and rub them all over with olive oil, then season. Sit them snugly in a small ovenproof dish. Cover with foil and roast in an oven preheated to 190ºC/375ºF/gas mark 5 for 1 hour 10 minutes. Then remove the foil, divide the butter between the onions and cook for another 25 minutes, basting with the melted butter a few times. Serve at once.

and also...

...melting roast onions with cheese

Cook the onions as above, then grate or slice 175g (6oz) cheese – slice if it's Brie, grate if it's Gruyère or Cheddar – and stuff it into the centre of the onions. Cook until the cheese melts for a great supper dish.

serves 4 as a side dish

250g (9oz) red lentils

½ tsp ground turmeric

1 x 2cm (¾in) square piece fresh root ginger, peeled and finely chopped

salt and pepper

4 tbsp sunflower oil

1 large onion, very finely sliced

2 garlic cloves, finely chopped

½ tbsp ground coriander

1 tbsp ground cumin

½ tsp cayenne pepper

juice of ½ small lemon

a fistful of coriander leaves, coarsely chopped

Tarka dhal shouldn't be too heavily flavoured; it is a mild background against which to highlight more strongly spiced food, and here the onions provide that. There's enough to serve two as a main course with chutneys, rice and plain yogurt, or serve as a side dish with an Indian spiced meat or chicken dish.

· · · · · ·

tarka dhal with crisp onions

I Put the lentils into a pan with the turmeric, ginger and seasoning and cover with water (about 500ml/18fl oz). Bring to the boil and partly cover with a lid. Turn the heat down and simmer the lentils for about 30 minutes. They should melt into a purée (you don't want the lentils to be too thick, so do add more water if you need to).

2 In the meantime, heat 3 tbsp of the sunflower oil and fry the onion over a medium-high heat for about 10 minutes; the edges should brown nicely. Add the rest of the oil and throw in the garlic and spices. Toss the onions around with the flavourings for a couple of minutes.

3 Season the lentils with salt, pepper and lemon. Pour into a warm serving dish and scatter the onions and the coriander on top.

Roasted, the tips of carrots, parsnips and onions caramelize and the flavour of beetroot intensifies. And just look at those colours!

serves 4 as a side dish

900g (2lb) squash or pumpkin

4 tbsp olive oil

25g (1oz) butter

salt and pepper

4 sprigs thyme

6 garlic cloves, finely sliced

Use the sweeter varieties of squash or pumpkin for this. The pale-green-skinned Crown Prince has a great flavour, and butternut squash is also very dependable.

. . . . . .

roast squash with garlic and thyme

I Halve the squash and scoop out and discard the seeds and fibres. Cut into slices about 2cm (¾in) thick at the thickest part. Put the olive oil and butter in a shallow roasting tin and heat gently. Add the wedges of squash and season well. Pull the leaves off the thyme and scatter those on, too, with some seasoning. Turn the wedges over, making sure you get herbs, fat and seasoning all over them. Put into an oven preheated to 190ºC/375ºF/gas mark 5 and roast for 30-35 minutes, or until tender and slightly caramelized. Baste the squash pieces every so often while they're cooking and sprinkle the garlic over 15 minutes before the end of cooking time.

and also...

...roast squash with chilli and ginger

Make as above, but sprinkle the squash slices with 2 shredded red chillies (halved and deseeded first) and finely chopped ginger (peel and chop a 5cm/2in square of fresh root ginger) 15 minutes before the end of cooking time.

Mmmm ... aniseed! This is a really fragrant treat but it is fairly rich so I always like to serve it with something quite plain, such as roast or grilled chicken or lamb.

・・・・・・

fennel and gruyère gratin

serves 4 as a side dish, 2 as a main course

4 fennel bulbs, trimmed of discoloured outer leaves

salt and pepper

butter, to grease

200ml (7fl oz) double cream

25g (1oz) Gruyère cheese, grated

25g (1oz) Parmesan, grated

I Trim the fennel tops and save any feathery fronds for later. Quarter each bulb lengthwise and boil the pieces in lightly salted boiling water for 4-5 minutes until nearly tender when pierced with the tip of a sharp knife. Drain well and lay the fennel in a buttered *gratin* dish, then sprinkle any reserved fronds on top. Season, pour on the cream and scatter with the cheeses. Bake in an oven preheated to 200°C/400°F/gas mark 6 for 20 minutes.

Not all autumn and winter veg dishes need to be cooked to softness and sweetness. Salads are also good, as long as they are not too delicate. This one is great for serving with fish or lamb.

・・・・・・

warm potato, fennel and olive salad

serves 6

900g (2lb) small waxy potatoes

salt and pepper

2 fennel bulbs

24 good-quality black olives

5 tbsp extra-virgin olive oil

juice of ½ lemon

I Cook the potatoes in boiling salted water until tender. While they're cooking, remove any tough outer leaves from the fennel and trim the tops, retaining any feathery fronds. Halve the fennel lengthwise and remove the little hard core from each piece and discard. Cut the fennel into very fine slices.

2 When the potatoes are tender, drain well and toss while still warm with the fennel, plus any fronds which you removed (chop these), olives, oil and lemon juice. Season. Serve warm or at room temperature.

Spanish cuisine boasts lots of bean dishes, slow-cooked with smoky *chorizo*, but they take ages. This one is good when you crave those textures and flavours without the wait.

. . . . . .

white beans and cabbage with chorizo

serves 4

200g (7oz) Savoy cabbage, about ½ medium-sized head

4 tbsp olive oil

2 garlic cloves, sliced

1 red chilli, halved, deseeded and finely sliced

150g (5½oz) *chorizo*, skin removed and cut into slices

1 x 410g (14½oz) can cannellini beans, drained, rinsed

salt and pepper

I Cut the cabbage in half. Remove the tough central white core from each piece and cut the leaves into slices about the thickness of your thumb.

2 Put half the olive oil into a frying pan with a lid. Add the garlic, chilli and *chorizo* and sauté until the garlic is pale gold and the *chorizo* coloured evenly. Toss in the cabbage and beans with the rest of the oil and season. Stir the vegetables around in the oil, then add a good splash of water. Turn down the heat, cover the pan and leave for 3 minutes, then give it all a stir and check that the beans are hot. Serve at once.

These smart beans are the perfect accompaniment for roast lamb or lamb chops. They're lovely with a couple of tablespoons of double cream stirred in and warmed through as well.

. . . . . .

flageolet beans with garlic and parsley

serves 6 as a side dish

20g (¾oz) butter

2 garlic cloves, finely chopped

2 x 400g (14oz) cans flageolet beans, drained and rinsed

2 tbsp finely chopped flat-leaf parsley

salt and pepper

I Melt the butter in a large saucepan and gently sauté the garlic until soft (just a couple of minutes). Add the beans, parsley and plenty of seasoning. Stir everything together until heated through.

spring and
summer fruit

● ● ● ● ● ● ●

Any red berries are good, particularly raspberries and loganberries. Currants and even blueberries work well, too.

· · · · · ·

summer berry brûlée

serves 6

700g (1lb 9oz) mixed raspberries and red and black currants

110g (4oz) caster sugar

300ml (10fl oz) whipping cream

295g (10½oz) Greek yogurt

175g (6oz) granulated sugar

I Put the fruit into a *gratin* dish (one that can take the heat of a grill) and sprinkle half the caster sugar all over it. Whip the cream and blend it with the Greek yogurt and the rest of the caster sugar. Spread the cream over the fruit. Cover with cling film and put in the refrigerator to chill well (the cream mixture firms up, which is really important).

2 Dust the granulated sugar evenly over the top of the cream and turn your grill to its highest setting. Grill the dish so that the sugar on top caramelizes – you may have to move it around a bit as most grills tend to be hotter in some patches and colder in others. Try to get it as evenly caramelized as possible. Remove from the grill and leave to come to room temperature. The sugar will set to a delicious crisp, sugary sheet – shiny and smooth enough to skate on – which contrasts brilliantly with the fruit.

Try to find good strawberries. Those big scarlet Elsantas you find on supermarket shelves look gorgeous but will leave you craving a proper strawberry flavour. Go instead for varieties such as Hapil and Cambridge Favourite, or the French Gariguette.

Sometimes you want a dessert just because of the idea of it. This is one of those puddings: golden eggy bread, tart raspberries, rich cream … Irresistible. If you can't get your hands on brioche – the sweet French bread – any good white bread will do as long as it has a soft crust.

· · · · · ·

pain perdu with clotted cream and raspberries

serves 4

150ml (5fl oz) double cream

2 large eggs, plus 1 large egg yolk

2 tbsp caster sugar

8 medium slices brioche

55g (2oz) unsalted butter

icing sugar, for dusting

175g (6oz) raspberries

clotted cream, to serve

I Whisk the cream and eggs together with the sugar. Either leave the brioche slices whole or cut them in half (a stack of four halves can look very good). Dunk the first two slices of brioche in the egg mix and leave for 5 minutes.

2 Melt a knob of the butter in a frying pan and cook the brioche slices, a couple at a time, adding more butter as you need to, until golden on each side. You need to dunk the next slices of brioche in the egg mixture as you go along. Put each slice on a paper towel as it is cooked.

3 Serve two slices of brioche per person, sift with icing sugar, and add the raspberries and clotted cream.

This is a very popular summer dessert in Sweden, where it's made with an almond paste called *mandelmass* (you can get it here but only in specialist Swedish shops). Marzipan works well instead, and you can use blueberries instead of raspberries.

. . . .

swedish baked peaches and raspberries with almonds

serves 6

8 ripe peaches, halved and stoned

250g (9oz) raspberries

75ml (2½fl oz) booze (ideally amaretto, Marsala, peach schnapps or even Cointreau)

juice of ½ small orange

2 tbsp caster sugar

200g (7oz) marzipan

15g (½oz) flaked almonds

icing sugar, for serving

I Cut each peach half into quarters and put them into a dish where they can be packed tightly together. Scatter the raspberries on top and pour on the alcohol and the orange juice. Sprinkle on half the sugar. Pull the marzipan into little nuggets, then scatter those on top of the fruit followed by the rest of the sugar and the flaked almonds.

2 Bake in an oven preheated to 190°C/375°F/gas mark mark 5 for 30–35 minutes. The peaches should be tender and slightly caramelized in patches. Leave to cool and serve warm or at room temperature, dusted lightly with icing sugar, with crème fraîche or Greek yogurt.

Many of the peaches and nectarines we get aren't great quality, and apricots are often 'woolly', but the application of heat and sugar does wonders for them. Baking concentrates their flavour, while lemon, almond and vanilla draw out their more elusive nuances.

You can use raspberries for this dish as well as strawberries. Basil's perfume goes well with them both.

. . . . . .

strawberries and pineapple in basil syrup

serves 6

225g (8oz) caster sugar

750ml (26fl oz) water

2 strips unwaxed lemon rind

4 large sprigs basil, torn, plus more leaves to serve

1 ripe pineapple

450g (1lb) strawberries

juice of ½ lemon

I Gently heat the sugar in the water with the strips of lemon rind, until the sugar has dissolved; boil for 15 minutes. Remove from the heat, add the basil and let the syrup infuse and cool.

2 Remove the skin from the pineapple and cut it into rounds. Divide each round into six little segments, removing the hard central core. Make sure that you remove any discoloured bits and any little bits of skin. Hull the strawberries and halve or quarter the larger ones.

3 Put the fruit into a serving bowl. Add the lemon juice to the basil syrup, then strain the syrup over the fruit. Put a sprig of fresh basil on top and serve.

A play on Eton Mess, that very English confection of crushed meringue, strawberries and cream.

. . . . . .

strawberry and passion-fruit mess

serves 6

400g (14oz) strawberries

7 passion-fruit

350ml (12fl oz) whipping cream

200g (7oz) Greek yogurt

juice of 1 lime

7 tbsp icing sugar

125g (4½oz) meringues

I Hull the strawberries and quarter or halve the largest ones. Halve the passion-fruit and extract the juice and seeds from all of them. Whip the cream, then add the yogurt, lime juice and sugar. Stir the strawberries and the passion-fruit (keeping back the smallest strawberries and some passion-fruit for decoration) into the cream.

2 Roughly smash up the meringues and gently fold them into the cream. Pile into glasses and garnish each one with a small strawberry and a drizzle of passion-fruit. Serve immediately.

serves 6

750ml (26fl oz) white wine

175g (6fl oz) caster sugar

2 strips unwaxed lemon rind

juice of ½ lemon

6 peaches, white ones if you can get them

2 tsp rosewater, or to taste

to serve

a small handful of pistachios, roughly chopped, *or*
deep-red rose petals, shredded or torn

Peaches are beautiful with pistachios and roses, so this is a gorgeous-looking dish. If you have perfectly ripe peaches that aren't too big, the peaches look good left whole, but halve and stone them if you prefer – it does make the cooking time quicker.

. . . . . .

peaches in rose syrup

I Put the wine, caster sugar and lemon rind and juice into a saucepan big enough to hold the peaches as well. Bring gently to the boil, stirring from time to time to help the sugar dissolve.

2 Leave the peaches whole and add them to the wine. Poach gently, turning them over every so often, until they are just tender. The length of time this takes depends on how ripe the peaches are. Remove the peaches and boil the poaching liquid until it is reduced and slightly syrupy. Leave to cool – the liquid will thicken more as it cools – then add the rosewater.

3 Carefully remove the skin from the peaches (it should just slip off) and halve them. Pour the syrup over the cooked peaches and chill. Throw some chopped pistachios or shredded rose petals over the top and serve.

and also...

...peaches in white wine and basil

Make as above but add a small bunch of basil leaves to the poaching liquid, then remove them once the syrup has cooled and use fresh leaves for serving. The basil flavour works well with red as well as white wine.

spring and summer fruit

147

Offer me baked apricots or half a dozen fancy pastries and I will choose this every time. The apricots we get here are rather woolly and lacking in flavour, but the wine, vanilla, sugar and heat somehow seem to reach into them and bring out their wonderful tart 'honeyedness'. Use good-quality vanilla extract if you don't have a pod. It won't look as pretty, but it will still taste good.

· · · · · ·

vanilla-baked apricots

serve 4

16 apricots, halved and stoned

250ml (9fl oz) white wine

1 vanilla pod, or 2 tsp vanilla extract

100g (3½oz) caster sugar

I Lay the apricots, skin-side up, in overlapping circles or rows in an ovenproof dish. Pour on the wine.

2 Split the vanilla pod and scrape out the seeds. Tuck the pod under the fruit and add the seeds to the white wine, agitating the dish to distribute them. Sprinkle with the sugar.

3 Bake in an oven preheated to 180°C/350°F/gas mark 4 for about 20–25 minutes, or until the apricots are tender and the sugar is very slightly caramelized. Allow to cool, then chill.

4 Serve with whipped cream, crème fraîche or slightly sweetened Greek yogurt and little Italian biscuits.

and also...

...cardamom-baked apricots

Make as above but add the seeds from 6 cardamom pods to the wine and leave out the vanilla. This is delicious served with plain Greek yogurt drizzled with a little honey and scattered with pistachios.

...lavender-baked apricots

Add 3 sprigs of fresh lavender to the wine and use fresh sprigs for serving. You can also replace some of the sugar with lavender honey.

...apricots in marsala

Replace the white wine with dry Marsala.

My standby summer pud. You can add blackberries or blackcurrants to the cooked fruit before serving.

• • • • • • •

cassis-baked fruit

serve 6

2 peaches or nectarines

4 plums

8 apricots

2 small apples

175ml (6fl oz) red wine

175ml (6fl oz) crème de cassis (blackcurrant liqueur)

55g (2oz) caster sugar

I Halve all the stone fruits. Cut the plums into quarters and the peaches into eighths. Core the apples and cut each half into six segments; I don't bother to peel them as I like the texture of the skin in the finished dish. Put the fruit into a shallow ovenproof dish and add all the other ingredients. Bake for 50 minutes in an oven preheated to 170ºC/325ºF/gas mark 3, stirring a couple of times if you get the chance. I like this best served with a big bowl of sweetened mascarpone cheese mixed with Greek yogurt.

When I was a teenager, one of my mother's most elegant friends produced, for pudding, a bowl of ripe peaches, a jug of cream and a silver sugar shaker. We watched as she carefully peeled her peach, sliced it, drizzled it with cream, dusted it with sugar and ate. It seemed like the perfect way to end a meal. With good food, it is sometimes best to do very little.

You can spend all summer never cooking a dessert at all, just serving fresh fruit. But as the months progress, fruit becomes abundant enough to take a less puristic approach. Keep it simple, though. Poached or baked fruit with subtle flavourings, such as flower waters or herbs, make the best eating.

Don't use rock-hard apricots here; you can bake hard apricots to softness but grilling them won't work. Keep the apricots in a bowl until they're tender. You can use blueberries if you can't find blackberries.

· · · · · ·

grilled apricots with blackberries and mascarpone

serves 4

12 ripe apricots, halved and stoned

75g (2½oz) caster sugar

125g (4½oz) mascarpone

75g (2½oz) blackberries

I Put the apricot halves, skin-side down, in a dish that can take the heat of a grill (such as a Le Creuset gratin dish). Sprinkle on a third of the sugar. Spoon the mascarpone into the hollows of the apricots and scatter the berries on and around the apricots. Sprinkle on another third of the sugar and put the dish under a very hot grill. Grill for 3 minutes. Sprinkle on the rest of the sugar and grill for another 3 minutes. The top should be glazed and bubbling. Serve immediately.

Gooseberries and elderflowers were made for each other, but I don't always want to be faffing around with sorbets or ice creams, so here is the taste of heaven in a good old-fashioned crumble.

· · · · · ·

gooseberry and almond crumble with elderflower cream

serves 8

900g (2lb) gooseberries, topped and tailed

125g (4½oz) caster sugar

125g (4½oz) plain flour

125g (4½oz) ground almonds

175g (6oz) butter, chopped

30g (1¼oz) flaked almonds

elderflower cream, to serve (see opposite)

I Put the gooseberries in an ovenproof serving bowl, and stir in 40g (1½oz) of the caster sugar. Add 50ml (2fl oz) water.

2 To make the crumble, mix the flour, the rest of the sugar and the ground almonds together. Rub in the butter until the mixture turns crumbly. Put the crumble on top of the gooseberries, scatter the flaked almonds over the top, and cook for about 40 minutes in an oven preheated to 180ºC/350ºF/gas mark 4. The top of the crumble should be golden. Leave to cool.

3 Serve with elderflower cream.

and also…

…raspberry, apple and almond crumble

Make as above, with 4 Bramley apples (peel and core them) and 500g (18oz) raspberries. Also good with elderflower cream, though you could try adding a little *crème de framboise* – raspberry liqueur – to the cream instead of elderflower cordial.

Delicious with clouds of meringue or good-quality shortbread. You can also make an orange or lemon cream by mixing the yogurt and cream with bought orange or lemon curd. (Duchy Originals curd is delicious.)

• • • • • •

poached rhubarb with elderflower cream

serves 4–6

900g (2lb) rhubarb

300ml (10fl oz) water

150g (5½oz) caster sugar

a good squeeze of lemon juice

elderflower cream

250g (9oz) Greek yogurt

100ml (3½fl oz) double cream

75g (2¾oz) icing sugar

a good squeeze of lemon juice

about 3 tbsp elderflower cordial, or to taste

I Trim the rhubarb and cut it into 6cm (2½in) lengths. Mix the water and sugar and heat, stirring from time to time, until the sugar has melted. Add the rhubarb to the sugar syrup and poach gently until just soft (the rhubarb must not collapse). Remove the rhubarb carefully with a slotted spoon and boil the poaching liquid to reduce it. The liquid should be slightly syrupy. Leave to cool and then add to the rhubarb. It's lovely chilled, so put it in the refrigerator.

2 To make the elderflower cream, beat the yogurt and double cream together. Add the other ingredients and mix well. (The cream will thicken when you add the lemon juice, but you will balance this out when you add the cordial. You should end up with a mixture that is firm but not stiff.) Cover and keep in the refrigerator until needed.

3 Serve the rhubarb in broad, shallow bowls, such as soup plates, with a good dollop of the cream.

A very grown-up dessert.

• • • • • •

raspberry and beaujolais granita

serves 8

600g (1lb 5oz) raspberries
150g (5½oz) caster sugar
175ml (6fl oz) Beaujolais

I Toss the raspberries in a bowl with 4 tbsp of the sugar. Leave for an hour. Heat the rest of the sugar in a saucepan with 150ml (5fl oz) of the wine, stirring to help the sugar dissolve. Boil for 2 minutes, then leave to cool.

2 Whiz the berries in a food processor. Push the purée through a sieve. Mix with the cooled syrup and the remaining wine. Chill. Freeze in a broad, shallow container. After 1½ hours, fork the bit that has frozen around the edge of the dish into the rest of the liquid. Fork about three more times (every 1½ to 2 hours) during the freezing, which will take about 8 hours in total. You want to break up the ice to make little shard-like crystals, not break them down as you would for a sorbet. If you make the *granita* the day before, put it in the refrigerator to defrost for about 20 minutes then fork it again before serving.

and also...

...gin and tonic *granita*
Gently heat 300ml (10fl oz) water and 300g (10½oz) caster sugar as above. Cool. Mix with the juice of 2 limes, the grated zest of 1 lime, 375ml (13fl oz) tonic water and 100ml (3½fl oz) gin. Continue as above.

...peach and *prosecco granita*
Make a sugar syrup as above, using 150ml (5fl oz) water and 150g (5½oz) caster sugar. Cool. Purée with the flesh of 4 ripe peaches. Sieve and mix with the syrup, the juice of 1½ lemons and 375ml (13fl oz) Prosecco. Continue as above. This is delicious with *crème de pêche* (French peach liqueur) poured over each serving.

The best meals end with elegance and simplicity. These make perfect finales when you're short of time.

· · · · · ·

no-cook puds

peaches with gorgonzola and mascarpone

This looks stunning and is a gorgeous combination of flavours. You need perfectly ripe, flavourful peaches (white-fleshed ones, if you can get them, are the most beautiful and scented). Leave some whole, halve or slice others and serve them on a platter with a wedge of Gorgonzola cheese, a bowl of mascarpone cheese and a generous chunk of honey on the comb.

peaches in moscato

A chic but lazy Italian dessert. Give every diner a glass of chilled Moscato (an Italian dessert wine, or French Muscat de Beaumes-de-Venise if you prefer) and a perfectly ripe peach. Let them peel their own peaches and cut them into slices, dropping each slice into the glass. Eat.

prosecco with sorbet and summer berries

Fill Champagne glasses with chilled Prosecco (not too much as it will froth once you add the sorbet). Drop a few red berries into the glasses and carefully top each one with a scoop of bought sorbet – mango or berry are good. Very glamorous.

figs and raspberries with mascarpone

Sounds plain, but the beauty of fresh figs makes this luxurious. Serve the figs whole on a large plate with the berries surrounding them and a big bowl of mascarpone cheese drizzled with good honey.

labneh with honey, pistachios and berries

Labneh is drained yogurt. For a sweet version you just mix plain Greek yogurt with some icing sugar and put it in a muslin- or J-cloth-lined sieve set over a bowl to drain overnight. Carefully remove the cloth and serve whole on a platter, or sliced into smaller wedges on individual plates. Drizzle with honey. Scatter with chopped pistachios and put red berries or slices of ripe peach, nectarine or mango alongside.

strawberries in beaujolais

Hull and wash strawberries and halve the larger ones. Put into a broad, shallow bowl and pour on enough Beaujolais to soak without covering. Sprinkle with caster sugar, gently stir and leave to macerate for 30 minutes before serving. You can use Valpolicella or a mixture of orange juice and Cointreau instead.

cherries on ice

There's nothing to this but it really sings of summer. Just wash the cherries – leaving the stalks on – and pile them into a bowl half-filled with ice-cubes.

boozy raisins

A good standby to keep in the cupboard. Put good raisins – such as Moscatel or Chilean Flame – into a big kilner jar, leaving room for the fruit to expand as it plumps up. Pour over enough booze (it should be something sweet, such as Madeira or Marsala) to cover the fruit completely, put the lid on and leave to plump up over a few days. Top up with more wine if the fruit starts to come up above the level of the liquid. Delicious with vanilla ice cream or big dollops of Greek yogurt or crème fraîche. Scatter the serving with toasted hazelnuts, pine nuts or almonds.

apricots in sauternes

Another good standby to have stashed in the cupboard. Pour a bottle of Sauternes (or you can use Muscat de Beaumes-de-Venise, Moscato or Moscatel) over 900g (2lb) dried apricots packed in a kilner jar. Cover and leave for at least a couple of weeks before eating. Top up with more wine if the fruit starts to come up above the level of the liquid. Scatter with toasted flaked almonds or chopped pistachios before serving.

prunes in armagnac

Richer and more boozy then the apricots above, so serve in smaller portions. Put 900g (2lb) very good-quality prunes into a kilner jar and cover with Armagnac or brandy. Cover and leave for at least a month before eating. You can do the same thing with dried figs. Both are great served alongside strong cheeses as well as a pudding.

chocolate-stuffed prunes

You can make these and stash them away, or prepare them very quickly. Get good-quality prunes. Make a slit in each one, remove the stone and stuff with chunks of dark chocolate and half a shelled walnut or a blanched almond. Make them more complicated if you wish, adding chopped candied peel or nuggets of marzipan to the mixture. Leave the prunes as they are or dip them in melted dark chocolate and allow to set. Beautiful if you can be bothered to wrap each one in tissue paper (go for fuchsia or purple paper – gorgeous.) Great with strong, dark espresso.

moroccan oranges with cinnamon

This only requires you to slice a few oranges but is a lovely, exotic and scented end to a winter meal. Prepare the slices according to the instructions on page 168. Lay the slices on a platter and pour any reserved juice over the top. Sprinkle with caster sugar (but taste first to see whether the oranges

need it or not) and a tbsp (or two – you judge, but don't make it too perfumed) of orange-flower water. Sprinkle on a little ground cinnamon and scatter with chopped pistachios. Chill before serving.

figs with goat cheese

The soft, bloomy skin of figs goes very well with goat cheese and they make a great combination. Make sure your figs are ripe and sweet and serve them whole, or cut them in quarters without cutting right through to the bottom so that they open out like flowers. Leave the goat cheese whole and serve on the same platter. Hazelnuts (shelled but not skinned) are lovely with this, too, as is a good honey.

feta-stuffed dates

Good for finishing off a Middle Eastern or North African meal. Just stone fresh or dried dates and stuff a nugget of feta cheese inside each one. You can add some slivers of pistachio as well if you want.

dark chocolate and pedro ximénez

You want really good-quality plain chocolate for this – something with over 70-percent cocoa solids – and you should get a good brand such as Valrhona or Green and Black's. Be generous. Simple desserts need to be abundant or you just look like a cheapskate. Serve with glasses of Pedro Ximénez, a sweet dessert sherry which tastes gorgeously of burnt sugar and raisins. (Honestly: sherry isn't just for the vicar!)

affogato

A simple ice-cream sundae for grown-ups. Make really good strong coffee, preferably espresso. Put a scoop of very cold, good-quality vanilla ice-cream into small bowls or coffee cups (it must be really cold). Pour a cupful of the hot coffee over the top of the ice-cream and serve immediately. You can fancy it up with a capful of liqueur if you like (Galliano and amaretto are nice).

autumn and winter fruit

· · · · · ·

One of the many apple puddings that are so popular in Scandinavia, this is from my Swedish friend, Johanna. It's not a tart, a crumble or a sponge, but it is incredibly easy and delicious and about the quickest pud you could make for Sunday lunch.

· · · · · ·

johanna's swedish apple pie

serves 8

125g (4½oz) butter, plus extra for greasing

5 eating apples, peeled and cored

150g (5½oz) caster sugar

200g (7oz) plain flour

¾ tsp baking powder

finely grated zest of 1 lemon

45g (1½oz) flaked almonds

to finish

icing sugar

I Butter an ovenproof dish. Cut the apples into wedges and lay them in the dish. Mix the sugar, flour, baking powder and lemon zest. Melt the butter and stir it into this, mixing well. Spread the mixture over the apples, and top with the almonds.

2 Bake in the middle of an oven preheated to 200°C/400°F/gas mark mark 6 for 30 minutes. Let the pudding cool slightly, then dust with icing sugar and serve.

Homely desserts – fat baked apples and juice-splattered crumbles – cheer everyone up. Why offer a bought cheesecake when a bowl of stewed apples and a jug of cream is so easy?

I generally find that cooking apples are a bit large to serve as a pudding, but eating apples are just the right size. You can fill them with honey, golden syrup, dried fruits and nuts and pour fruit juice, cider or sherry around them.

· · · · · ·

new england baked apples

serves 4

4 large eating apples

55g (2oz) dried cranberries or raisins (or a mixture)

55g (2oz) pecan pieces

55g (2oz) fresh cranberries

125ml (4fl oz) maple syrup, plus extra for drizzling

150ml (5fl oz) cider or fruit juice

I Make a 'lid' out of the top of each apple by cutting around the stem (make each one about 5cm/2in across). Set the lids aside and remove the core from the rest of the apple with a corer.

2 Mix together everything else except the cider. Place the apples in an ovenproof dish and spoon the stuffing into them. Put the lids on and drizzle some maple syrup over each apple. Pour the cider or juice into the dish around the apples and bake in an oven preheated to 180°C/ 350°F/gas mark 4 for 30-40 minutes. The apples should be tender. Spoon the juice over the apples every so often while they are cooking. Serve warm with crème fraîche.

and also...

...marmalade-baked apples

Mix 4 tbsp flaked almonds, 4 tbsp sultanas or raisins, 3 tbsp marmalade and 2 tbsp golden syrup and stir in the juice of ½ orange. Fill the apples as above, top with a tsp marmalade and a tbsp golden syrup. Pour in the juice of 1½ oranges and bake as above.

...swedish baked apples with tosca sauce

Dot little knobs of butter and sprinkle 2 tbsp caster sugar over 4 halved and cored apples and bake in an oven preheated to 200°C/400°F/gas mark 6 for 30 minutes. In a small saucepan, mix 55g (2oz) butter, 55g (2oz) caster sugar, 1 tbsp plain flour, 55g (2oz) flaked almonds and 4 tbsp double cream and heat carefully, stirring until it thickens. Pour over the apples and bake for another 10 minutes, until they're tender and golden.

If you don't have stale cake to hand and can't find brioche, you can use any sweet bread or fruit loaf to make the crumbs for this. A great pud for Saturday or Sunday lunch.

· · · · · ·

rhubarb and apple brown betty

serves 6

225g (8oz) light brown sugar

½ tsp ground mixed spice and ½ tsp ground ginger

100g (3½oz) stale plain cake or brioche crumbs

85g (3oz) butter, melted, plus extra for greasing

500g (18oz) rhubarb, trimmed and cut into 2cm (¾in) lengths

2 cooking apples, peeled, cored and thinly sliced

4 tbsp orange juice

I Mix the sugar and spices together. Put 3 tbsp into the crumbs and stir in the melted butter.

2 Toss the fruit with the rest of the sugar-and-spice mix. Butter a shallow pie dish and spread half the crumbs in the base. Pile the fruit on top and pour in the juice. Put the rest of the crumbs on top and bake, loosely covered with foil, in an oven preheated to 180°C/350°F/gas mark 4 for 20 minutes. Remove the foil and bake for another 20 minutes, until golden. Serve with whipped cream or vanilla ice cream.

Fools can be rich so they're best made with really tart fruit. You could use half cream, half Greek yogurt instead of cream and custard, but you'll need to add more sugar.

· · · · · ·

apple, maple and ginger fool

serves 4

800g (1¾lb) Bramley apples, peeled

25g (1oz) soft light brown sugar

2 globes preserved ginger in syrup, chopped, plus 1 tbsp ginger syrup from the jar

150ml (5fl oz) whipping cream

300g (10½oz) fresh custard (bought is fine)

5 tbsp dark maple syrup, plus more for drizzling

I Cut the apples into chunks, discarding the cores, and put in a saucepan with 2 tbsp water and the sugar. Heat gently, then simmer until the apples are completely soft and mushy. Leave to cool.

2 Purée the apples with the ginger and ginger syrup. Whip the cream until it holds soft peaks. Carefully mix the apple purée, cream, custard and maple syrup together and chill. Serve in a large bowl or in individual glasses, drizzled with maple syrup.

serves 4

2 perfectly ripe, medium mangoes, peeled

6 passion-fruit

juice of 4 limes and finely grated zest of 2

caster sugar

150ml (5fl oz) double cream

5 tbsp white rum

Thank goodness for tropical fruits: they're at their best during our winter months. Mangoes, which don't have much natural acidity, really sing out when teamed with the tartness of passion-fruit or lime juice. You don't have to limit the combination to this dish, of course; mango and passion-fruit are also great with cold rice pudding, or combined with segments of orange for a simple fruit compote to serve with whipped cream.

· · · · · ·

mangoes and passion-fruit with rum and lime syllabub

I Cut off the 'cheeks' of the mangoes by slicing through the flesh on either side of the central stone, so that you are left with two rounded fleshy sides and a stone, which still has quite a lot of fruit on it. Cut the cheeks into neat slices. Cut as much of the fruit off the stone as you can. Keep any odd slices or squashed bits for other things, like a breakfast smoothie, or eat them as a cook's perk.

2 Halve the passion-fruit and scoop out the pulp and seeds. Toss the mango slices with the juice of 2 limes, ½ tbsp caster sugar and most of the passion-fruit (keep some back for decoration). Cover and chill for about 10 minutes. If you leave it much longer, the lime softens the mango flesh too much.

3 Whip the cream with the lime zest, adding the rest of the lime juice and the rum at intervals. Don't overbeat. The cream should fall in soft folds. Add caster sugar to taste.

4 Put the fruit into 4 glasses and spoon the syllabub on top. Finish with a drop of passion-fruit on top of the cream.

and also...

...mangoes with ginger, mint and lemon grass
Put 140ml (4½fl oz) water, 125g (4½oz) caster sugar, a 2.5cm (1in) cube fresh root ginger (peeled and sliced), 1 lemon grass stalk (bruised and chopped) and the juice of 2 limes into a saucepan and slowly bring to the boil. Cook for 7 minutes and add a handful of mint leaves. Let the syrup infuse as it cools, then strain it and chill. Prepare 2 mangoes as above, cutting off the cheeks. You are only going to use the cheeks for this, so save the rest of the flesh for something else. Lay the cheeks on a cutting board and cut each one in slices, holding on to the mango flesh so that it stays together in the cheek shape. Carefully place each sliced cheek in a broad, shallow bowl and pour the syrup over the slices. Add a handful of small mint leaves and serve cold.

This makes a lovely, rustic-looking, dark and glossy pudding. If you can't find Moscatel – an inexpensive Spanish dessert wine – use Marsala or medium sherry instead. Roughly chopped hazelnuts or almonds will do just as well as pine nuts.

. . . . . .

pears, raisins and pine nuts baked in moscatel

serves 6

70g (2½oz) raisins

250ml (9fl oz) Moscatel

6 slightly under-ripe pears, halved and cored

50ml (2fl oz) water

juice of 1 lemon

40g (1½oz) soft light or dark brown sugar

20g (¾oz) pine nuts

I Put the raisins in a small saucepan and pour on the Moscatel. Bring to just under the boil, then leave the raisins to plump up for about 30 minutes.

2 Lay the pears, cut-side up, in a single layer in a shallow ovenproof dish. Spoon the raisins around them – if they're put on top, they will burn. Pour on the Moscatel, water and lemon juice. Sprinkle the sugar on top of the pears and around them. Put the dish in an oven preheated to 180°C/350°F/gas mark 4, and bake for 45 minutes, or until the pears are tender and starting to wrinkle at the edges. From time to time, spoon the juices over the top. Add the pine nuts midway through cooking.

3 Serve at room temperature with crème fraîche or Greek yogurt.

and also...

...baked pears stuffed with chocolate and hazelnuts
Halve and core 6 pears, then crush 3 digestive biscuits, 85g (3oz) hazelnuts and 2 tbsp soft light brown sugar together. Add a small beaten egg and 85g (3oz) chopped dark chocolate. Spoon the filling into the core cavities and over the pears, sprinkle with 40g (1½oz) soft light brown sugar and nuggets of butter (use about 15g/½oz). Bake as above, with 250ml (9fl oz) sweet wine, 50ml (2fl oz) water and the juice of 1 lemon poured around the pears. Scatter on coarsely chopped toasted hazelnuts.

Use crimson-fleshed plums if you can —
they look beautiful. Good for both
pudding and afternoon tea.

· · · · · ·

plum and hazelnut cake

As well as using seasonal
fruit for crumbles and
cakes, ring the changes
by adding dried stuff:
apricots, plums and sour
cherries. And don't forget
fresh cranberries.

serves 8

8-10 large red or purple plums, halved and stoned

125g (4½oz) butter, softened and diced, plus extra
for buttering

100g (3½oz) caster sugar, plus 1 extra tbsp

3 medium eggs, lightly beaten

finely grated zest of 1 lemon

100g (3½oz) self-raising flour, sifted

100g (3½oz) toasted hazelnuts, ground, keeping back some
of the coarser bits in the mixture for decoration

2 tbsp whole milk

I Cut each plum half into 3 slices. Butter a 20cm (8in)
springform tin and line the base with greaseproof paper.

2 Put the butter, sugar (minus the extra tbsp), eggs,
lemon zest, flour, nuts and milk into a food processor
and whiz until smooth. Spoon the batter into the tin and
arrange the plum slices, cut-side up, in circles on top.
Make sure you pack them well together. Sprinkle with
1 tbsp caster sugar (or more if the plums are very tart)
and bake in an oven preheated to 180°C/350°F/gas mark
4 for 40 minutes. A skewer inserted into the centre of the
cake should come out clean.

3 Let the cake cool in its tin for 15 minutes, then remove
it, peeling off the greaseproof paper on the bottom, and
put it on a wire rack to cool completely.

and also...

...pear and walnut cake
Make the cake the same way as above but replace the hazelnuts with walnuts and
the plums with three pears. Cut the cored pears into about 1cm (½in) thick slices
and lay them any way you like over the cake batter.

An easy autumnal trifle. You don't
even need any cake!

• • • • • •

plum and
ginger trifle

serves 6

500g (18oz) plums, halved and stoned

75ml (2½fl oz) water

100g (3½oz) soft light brown sugar

½ knob preserved ginger in syrup, finely chopped, plus
1 tbsp ginger syrup from the jar

150g (5½oz) ginger biscuits, plus 2 extra biscuits,
crushed, for decoration

40ml (1½fl oz) whisky

55g (2oz) shelled walnuts, roughly chopped,
plus a few extra for decoration

450ml (16fl oz) double cream

6 tbsp Greek yogurt

6 tbsp icing sugar

I Put the plums and water in a pan with the brown sugar
and chopped ginger. Bring to the boil, stirring a little to
help the sugar dissolve, then simmer for 15-20 minutes,
depending on the ripeness of the plums, until the plums
have completely collapsed and the mixture is quite thick.
If your mixture is too runny, keep simmering and it will
thicken as it reduces. Add the ginger syrup and leave to
cool completely.

2 Roughly break up the ginger biscuits. Sprinkle the
whisky on them and mix with the walnuts. Whip the
cream, beating in the yogurt, and add the icing sugar.

3 Layer the components in a large glass bowl or in
small glasses, finishing with some cream. Cover and
leave in the refrigerator for a couple of hours or until
the following day. Just before serving, sprinkle on the
reserved ginger biscuits and walnuts.

autumn and winter fruit

167

Don't think this is ordinary;
it's a stunning-looking dessert. The
colours of the fruits sparkle together –
just as the rosemary works beautifully
with the citrus-fruit flavours.

· · · · · ·

citrus fruit and rosemary compote

serves 6

275ml (9½fl oz) freshly squeezed orange juice

175ml (6fl oz) water

175g (6oz) caster sugar

3 sprigs of rosemary

juice of ½ lemon

2 oranges

3 blood oranges

1 grapefruit

1 ruby grapefruit

I Heat the orange juice with the water, sugar and 1 sprig of rosemary, stirring to help the sugar dissolve. Bring to the boil, then simmer for about 20 minutes until slightly syrupy, leaving about 300ml (10fl oz) liquid. Add the lemon juice and other rosemary sprigs. Leave to cool.

2 Cut a slice from both the top and bottom of the fruits so that there is a flat base at each end. Remove the peel and pith by setting the fruits on one of their flat bases and cutting from top to bottom, following the curve of the fruit and working your way around it.

3 Now cut each fruit into thin slices. Pick out any seeds and throw them away. Put the fruit in a shallow bowl (plain white or glass is lovely), pour over the citrus syrup with the rosemary sprigs and chill.

4 Serve with sweetened crème fraîche or whipped cream. Little almond biscuits are very good on the side.

and also...

...spiced orange and red wine compote

In a saucepan, heat 500ml (18fl oz) red wine, 250ml (9fl oz) orange juice, 200g (7oz) caster sugar, 3 star anise, 1 cinnamon stick and 3 strips each of lemon and orange rind. Stir to help the sugar dissolve. Bring to the boil, simmer for 12 minutes, then cool completely. Add 2 tbsp Cointreau if you want. Prepare 9 oranges as above. Remove the rind from the syrup, then pour it over the orange slices. Chill to serve.

12 figs, not too ripe

35g (1¼oz) plain chocolate, cut into little chunks

20g (¾oz) shelled walnuts, roughly chopped

55g (2oz) marzipan, cut into little chunks

300ml (10fl oz) red wine

55g (2oz) caster sugar, plus an extra 3 tbsp for sifting

1½ tbsp crème de cassis (blackcurrant liqueur)

to serve

200g (7oz) Greek yogurt

55g (2oz) mascarpone cheese

icing sugar, to taste

Although I'd usually serve three figs per person, this is such a rich filling you only need two. It's better to use slightly under-ripe figs; they can withstand the cooking without falling apart.

. . . . . .

marzipan and chocolate stuffed figs in red-wine syrup

I Trim the tip off each fig. Cut a cross in the top but don't slice right through – you want to end up with a fig that just gently opens like a flower. Press the fig open and stuff each one with the chocolate, nuts and marzipan until you've used everything up. Carefully push the figs back into shape, without squeezing out the stuffing. Place them in a small ovenproof dish where they'll all fit snugly.

2 Put the wine and the 55g (2oz) caster sugar into a saucepan and heat gently, stirring a little to help the sugar dissolve. Turn the heat up and boil the liquid until it's reduced by a third. Add the cassis. Pour the syrup round the figs, spooning a little of it over each fruit, then sprinkle with the extra sugar (this will just help it to caramelize a little). Put the figs into an oven preheated to 180°C/350°F/gas mark 4, and cook for 20 minutes. The figs should be soft, but not collapsing.

3 Mix the yogurt and mascarpone together. Add icing sugar to taste (remember that you're serving it with something very sweet). Leave the cooked figs to cool a little and serve either warm or at room temperature with the cream.

A cheat's pudding, since it involves doctoring some bought vanilla ice cream, but it's none the worse for that. Just make sure not to let the ice cream go as far as melting when you are trying to soften it – melted and refrozen ice cream can cause food poisoning.

Turrón is Spanish nougat. If you can't find it, any nougat will do.

· · · · · · ·

figs baked in sherry with honey and turrón ice cream

serves 6

18 fresh figs, not too ripe

225ml (8fl oz) sweet sherry, plus 2 extra tbsp

5 tbsp soft light brown sugar

finely grated zest of 1 small orange

125g (4½oz) soft *turrón*, or Italian nougat

700ml (1¼ pints) good-quality vanilla ice cream

2 tbsp runny honey

I Halve the figs and pour 200ml (7fl oz) of the sherry into a shallow *gratin* dish. Add 3 tbsp of the sugar and all of the orange rind. Set the figs, cut-side up, in the sherry. Drizzle the other 25ml (1fl oz) of the sherry over the top and sprinkle on the rest of the sugar.

2 Roast for 15-20 minutes in an oven preheated to 190°C/375°F/gas mark 5, until the figs are soft and the tops slightly caramelized. Let the figs cool.

3 Cut the *turrón* into little chunks. Slightly soften the vanilla ice cream and stir in the honey and the *turrón*, mixing well. Quickly get the ice cream back into the freezer to chill and firm up.

4 Pour the extra 2 tbsp sherry over the figs once they're cooked (it just heightens the sherry flavour) and serve them, warm or at room temperature, with the ice cream.

Cold-weather puds don't have to be tawny in colour. Autumn brings scarlet cranberries, crimson pomegranates and purple figs, and citrus fruits are at their best during winter.

Granitas may seem too cold for autumn and winter, but sometimes after a plate of filling comfort food it's exactly what you need. Frosted glasses filled with colourful shards of ice can look spectacular, too.
It's now possible to find bottles of pure pomegranate juice (such as Pom Wonderful) quite easily. If blood oranges aren't in season, you can use a carton of squeezed juice.

· · · · · ·

pomegranate, blood orange and campari granita

serves 6

300ml (10fl oz) pomegranate juice

200ml (7fl oz) blood-orange juice

juice of 1 lemon

75g (2¾oz) caster sugar

7 tbsp Campari

pomegranate seeds (optional)

I Heat everything together gently, except the Campari and seeds, stirring a little to help the sugar dissolve. Leave to cool then add the Campari. Pour into a shallow container and freeze, roughly forking the mixture about four times during the freezing process which will take about 12 hours.

2 Spoon into glasses and sprinkle some pomegranate seeds on top if you want.

and also...

...cranberry and port *granita*

Put 350g (12oz) fresh cranberries into a pan with 300ml (10fl oz) water. Bring to the boil and simmer for about 5 minutes, or until the fruit is soft. Push the fruit through a sieve and leave to cool. In another pan, heat 500g (18oz) caster sugar and 500ml (18fl oz) water, stirring a little to help the sugar dissolve, then simmer for 5 minutes. Leave this to cool then mix it with the fruit purée and 7 tbsp port. Continue as above.

...apple and calvados *granita*

Put 600ml (20fl oz) water and 150g (5½oz) caster sugar in a pan, and heat gently until the sugar has dissolved. Add 450g (1lb) peeled and chopped apple flesh (from eating apples) and cook until soft. Cool and whiz in a food processor with the juice of ½ lemon and 5 tbsp Calvados (or brandy). Continue as above. Serve in chilled glasses with more Calvados poured over each serving.

700g (1lb 9oz) Bramley apples (about 4), peeled, cored and chopped

300g (10½oz) blackberries

185g (6½oz) caster sugar

a slug of crème de cassis or *crème de mûre* (blackcurrant or blackberry liqueurs), optional

75g (2¾oz) plain flour

75g (2¾oz) wholemeal flour

150g (5½oz) cold butter, cut into cubes

150g (5½oz) soft dark brown sugar

55g (2oz) brown breadcrumbs

75g (2¾oz) shelled hazelnuts

Crumbles are all very well but – and this may sound sacrilegious – in autumn and winter I like them nutty, with a flavour of burnt sugar. This one is the business. You can use walnuts or pecans here, too, or a mixture of nuts. I grew up in the countryside, where blackberry-picking was just something you did, but it's harder to get your hands on them in the city. If you're making this outside blackberry season or simply can't find any, use blackberries canned in natural fruit juice instead. Just drain them.

I Put the apples and blackberries into a pie dish and add the caster sugar. Mix to make sure all the fruit gets coated and drizzle on a little of the liqueur, if using.

2 In a food processor, pulse together the flours, butter and sugar until the mixture looks like breadcrumbs. Add the breadcrumbs. Chop the hazelnuts very roughly – some should be left whole, in fact; you want a good chunky crumble – and add them to the flour mixture. Pat the crumble mixture on top of the fruit and bake in an oven preheated to 180ºC/350ºF/gas mark 4 for 35-40 minutes. The fruit should be completely tender and the top brown and bubbling.

· · · · · ·

hedgerow crumble

Flavoured creams are wonderful for jazzing up simple cakes or fruit. The quantities of flavouring and sugar given are guidelines only. You need to adjust them, depending on what they're being served with. Add the flavourings as the cream starts to hold its shape. Adding anything acidic, such as lemon juice, will immediately thicken cream further.

· · · · · ·

flavoured creams

ginger and lime cream

Beat 300ml (10fl oz) whipping or double cream with 2 tbsp ginger marmalade and some finely chopped preserved ginger. When it's stiffening, beat in the juice and grated zest of 2 limes. It shouldn't need sweetening, but add soft light brown sugar if you like. Good with sliced mangoes or a mixture of melons.

brown-sugar cream

Stir 4 tbsp double cream into 400g (14oz) Greek yogurt. Sprinkle with 100g (3½oz) soft dark brown sugar. You can either leave this to form a soft dark crust, or gently stir it in to marble the mixture. Great with stewed or baked apples and warm ginger cake.

maple cream

Beat 300ml (10fl oz) double or whipping cream and add 4-5 tbsp dark maple syrup. Squeeze in a good bit of lemon juice and stir. Taste to see if you want to adjust anything. Very good with apple and pear puds.

cassis cream

Beat 300ml (10fl oz) double or whipping cream and stir in 2 tbsp icing sugar and 5 tbsp crème de cassis (blackcurrant liqueur). Good with plain red berries.

marmalade and orange-flower cream

Beat 300ml (10fl oz) double or whipping cream and, as it starts to thicken, add 75g (2¾oz) marmalade. The beaters will break it up. Beat in 1 tbsp orange-flower water and add icing sugar to taste. You can also add whisky to this instead of the flower water. Great with chocolate or orange cake.

elderflower cream

Beat 250g (9oz) Greek yogurt and 100ml (3½fl oz) double cream together. Add 4 tbsp icing sugar and a good squeeze of lemon juice. Stir in 4 tbsp elderflower cordial. Taste and adjust accordingly (elderflower cordials vary in strength). Good with poached gooseberry and rhubarb puddings.

passion-fruit cream

Scoop the pulp and seeds out of 4 passion-fruit. Sieve this and remove half the seeds. Add the rest back to the fruit pulp. Beat 300ml (10fl oz) double or whipping cream until it's just holding its shape, then add the passion-fruit and 3 tbsp icing sugar. This is surprisingly good with raspberries and strawberries.

lemon curd mascarpone

Beat 125g (4½oz) mascarpone cheese to loosen it. Stir in 75g (2¾oz) fromage frais and 250g (9oz) good-quality lemon curd. Good with a cake, such as the rhubarb one on page 183, or with big meringues.

boozy cream

Beat 300ml (10fl oz) double or whipping cream and, as it starts to thicken, beat in 4 tbsp Calvados, amaretto, Bourbon, Marsala, kirsch or whisky, and 4 tbsp icing, caster or soft light brown sugar. Pick your booze to suit the pudding or cake it's to go with.

flour, eggs
sugar, cream

· · · · · ·

I love cakes that can be just mixed with a wooden spoon and bunged in the oven. Try orange-blossom water here instead of rosewater. An orange-scented version is good with peach or apricot compote.

· · · · · ·

rose-drenched yogurt cake with summer berries

serves 8

200g (7oz) self-raising flour, sifted

115g (4oz) ground almonds

150g (5½oz) caster sugar

a good pinch of salt

1 tsp baking powder

2 large eggs, beaten

250g (9oz) plain Greek yogurt

150ml (5fl oz) sunflower oil

finely grated zest of 1 lime

syrup

275ml (9½fl oz) water

175g (6oz) caster sugar

juice of 2 limes

1 tbsp rosewater

to serve

icing sugar

summer berries (raspberries and blueberries are great)

crème fraîche or Greek yogurt

I To make the syrup, put the water, sugar and lime juice into a saucepan. Heat gently, stirring to help the sugar dissolve. Bring to the boil and simmer for 7 minutes. Leave to cool, then add the rosewater.

2 Tip all the dry ingredients for the cake into a bowl and make a well in the centre. Add the rest of the ingredients and mix with a wooden spoon. Pour into a buttered 20cm (8in) springform cake tin and bake in an oven preheated to 180°C/350°F/gas mark mark 4 for 30 minutes. A skewer inserted into the middle of the cake should come out clean.

3 Let the cake cool in the tin for 10 minutes, then turn out onto a plate. Pierce it all over with a skewer and pour the syrup over the warm cake. Dust with icing sugar just before serving (otherwise the sugar sinks into the syrupy top) and serve with berries and crème fraîche.

flour, eggs, sugar, cream

serves 8

125g (4½oz) self-raising flour, sifted

a pinch of salt

55g (2oz) cocoa powder

3 large eggs, beaten

175g (6oz) caster sugar

175g (6oz) butter, slightly softened and diced, plus extra for buttering

2 drops vanilla extract

4 tbsp warm water

icing

150g (5½oz) good-quality plain chocolate, broken into small pieces

75ml (2½fl oz) sour cream

75ml (2½fl oz) double cream

5 tbsp soft dark brown sugar

decoration

toasted hazelnuts (a few whole, the rest halved or quartered) or toasted flaked almonds

icing sugar (optional)

An easy-to-do chocolate cake that you can quickly whip up for friends or children's birthday parties. If you're making it for children, you might prefer to use milk chocolate instead of plain chocolate for the icing, in which case you can sweeten the glaze with caster sugar or sifted icing sugar rather than dark brown sugar.

. . . . . .

all-in-one chocolate cake

I Put all the ingredients for the cake, except the water, into a food processor or a bowl in which you can beat the ingredients with an electric whisk. Whiz or beat until combined. Add the water and mix again. Put into a buttered 20cm (8in) springform cake tin and bake for 25-30 minutes in an oven preheated to 190°C/375°F/gas mark 5. The cake is ready when a skewer inserted into the middle comes out clean. Turn out and leave to cool.

2 To make the icing, put everything in a bowl set over a pan of simmering water and allow to melt. Stir everything together, take off the heat and leave to cool and thicken. Spread this over the cake with a palette knife, then decorate with nuts and sift over a light dusting of icing sugar if desired.

A version of the near-miraculous and eternally popular Australian lemon pudding – miraculous because, as the pudding cooks, a luscious layer of sauce forms beneath the sponge. Couldn't be simpler.

· · · · · ·

baked lime and passion-fruit pudding

serves 6

60g (2¼oz) butter, softened and diced

300g (10½oz) caster sugar

finely grated zest and juice of 2 limes

3 large eggs, separated

5 tbsp self-raising flour

350ml (12fl oz) milk

3 ripe passion-fruit

icing sugar, to serve

I Throw the butter, sugar and zest into a food processor and process until light and fluffy. Add the egg yolks and blend, then add the flour, alternating with the milk. Blend until you have a smooth batter. Add the lime juice.

2 Halve the passion-fruit and scoop out the pulp and seeds. Remove and discard about a third of the black seeds (you can sieve the pulp and add two-thirds of the seeds back into the pulp) and add the pulp and seeds to the batter. Pour the batter into a large bowl.

3 Beat the egg whites until stiff but not dry and, using a large metal spoon, fold into the batter. Spoon into a buttered 1 litre (36fl oz) pudding dish and set in a roasting tin. Pour boiling water into the roasting tin to come about halfway up the sides of the pudding dish. Bake in an oven preheated to 180°C/350°F/gas mark 4 for 1 hour.

4 Allow to cool a little when it comes out of the oven. Sift some icing sugar over the top and serve with thick cream.

Torrijas are basically Spanish French-toast, if that makes any sense, or 'eggy bread' in down-to-earth English. They treat *torrijas* with some respect in Spain; it's not just a way of getting rid of a stale old loaf. This is a particularly classy treatment and makes an easy dessert. (Or have *torrijas* for breakfast if you feel like being a pig.)

I can't remember where I first came across honey ambrosia, but you always see jars of honey and nuts for sale in Italy and Greece for ridiculous prices. This, since you're making it, is cheaper. It's also better. Use decent honey and make sure the nuts aren't old. You can use dried apricots, chopped, instead of raisins, or a mixture of the two. The recipe makes more ambrosia than you need for four people, but just keep the rest for the next time (or have it on Greek yogurt for breakfast).

· · · · · ·

torrijas with honey ambrosia

serves 4

ambrosia

40g (1½oz) raisins, preferably a really good variety such as Moscatel or Lexia

5 tbsp medium-sweet sherry

85g (3oz) hazelnuts and blanched almonds, toasted and very roughly chopped (you want some good big chunks and halved nuts in the mixture)

250g (9oz) honey

torrijas

2 large eggs, plus 1 large egg yolk

6 tbsp double cream

2 tbsp caster sugar

2 tbsp sweet sherry

4 thick slices soft white bread or brioche

55g (2oz) unsalted butter

icing sugar, to dust

I To make the ambrosia, put the raisins and the sherry in a small saucepan. Heat gently, then leave the raisins to plump up for anything from 30 minutes to 24 hours.

2 Add the nuts and honey to the raisin and sherry mix in the saucepan and heat until bubbling. Simmer for 3-4 minutes. Pour into a sauce boat, if you're going to use it immediately, or into a sterilized jam jar to store it.

3 For the *torrijas*, beat the eggs with the cream, sugar and sherry in a wide, shallow bowl. Cut each slice of bread in half and coat the pieces in the egg mix, then leave them for about 5 minutes to absorb the liquid. This will give you lighter *torrijas*.

4 Melt the butter in a large frying pan until foaming and cook the bread for about 3 minutes on each side until golden brown. Serve each person with 2 pieces of bread, dusted with icing sugar and drizzled with the ambrosia. Crème fraîche or Greek yogurt cuts the sweetness – especially if you're serving it for breakfast or brunch.

flour, eggs, sugar, cream

This is a good blueprint to use for other fruit-topped cakes. Instead of rhubarb you could try sliced peaches, nectarines, plums, pears or apricots. You just need to make sure your fruit is tender and ripe – any hard, unripe fruit won't soften in the half hour it takes the cake batter to cook.

· · · · · ·

rhubarb cake

serves 8

125g (4½oz) butter, softened and diced, plus extra for buttering

125g (4½oz) caster sugar, plus 5 tbsp for the rhubarb

3 large eggs, beaten

2 tsp vanilla extract

125g (4½oz) self-raising flour, sifted

2–3 tbsp milk

700g (1lb 9oz) rhubarb, trimmed and cut into 2.5cm (1in) lengths

icing sugar, to dust

1 Beat the butter and sugar together until pale and fluffy. Add the eggs a little at a time, beating well after each addition. If the mixture starts to curdle, add a tbsp of the flour. Add the vanilla, then fold in the flour with a large metal spoon, adding enough of the milk to give the batter a reluctant dropping consistency. Scrape into a buttered 20cm (8in) springform cake tin.

2 Toss the rhubarb with the 5 tbsp sugar and spread it over the top of the cake mixture. Bake for 40 minutes in an oven preheated to 190ºC/375ºF/gas mark 5. The rhubarb will be slightly singed in parts. The cake is ready when a skewer inserted into the middle comes out clean.

3 Leave the cake to cool in the tin, then carefully remove the ring and base. Dust with icing sugar before serving.

Baking doesn't mean you have to don a pinny and slave over a state-of-the-art food mixer. There are plenty of cakes for which you need nothing more than scales and a wooden spoon or hand mixer.

I am very bad at baked rice pudding. Somehow I always manage to use either not enough milk or too much, so now I do this stove-top version. It's a doddle, and quicker to make than the oven-baked version, too.

. . . . . .

chilled rice pudding with orange, honey and cardamom syrup

and also...

...with sour cherries in rose syrup

Put 150g (5½oz) caster sugar and 300ml (10fl oz) dry white wine in a saucepan and heat gently, then bring to the boil and simmer for 5 minutes. Add 200g (7oz) dried sour cherries. Let the fruit simmer for 2-3 minutes, then take the pan off the heat. Add the juice of 1 lime and ½ tbsp rosewater. Allow to cool. You can serve the cherries at room temperature or chill them.

...with pomegranate and blood-orange sauce

Squeeze the juice from 1 pomegranate (do it just as if it were an orange) and put it into a saucepan with 175ml (6fl oz) blood-orange juice, 2 strips of orange rind and 85g (3oz) caster sugar. Gently bring to the boil, then simmer for 5 minutes. Leave the syrup to cool, remove the orange rind and add the seeds of 2 pomegranates.

serves 4

150g (5½oz) short-grain rice
900ml (32fl oz) full-fat milk
35g (1¼oz) caster sugar
100ml (3½fl oz) thick double cream
3 tbsp Greek yogurt
a couple of drops of vanilla extract

syrup

6 tbsp honey
3 tbsp water
juice of 2 oranges
crushed seeds from 4 cardamom pods
finely grated zest of 1 orange

1 Put the rice in a saucepan and cover it with water. Boil for 4 minutes, then drain. Put the rice back in the pan with the milk and sugar and bring to the boil, then turn down to a simmer. Cook for 20-30 minutes, until all the liquid has been absorbed and the rice is soft. You need to stir from time to time and add a little more milk if you find it has been absorbed before the rice is soft.

2 Take the pan off the heat. Stir half the cream and yogurt and all the vanilla into the rice. Taste to check the sweetness, bearing in mind that the syrup is sweet. Leave to cool, then chill. When chilled, the pudding will be very firm, so before serving, loosen it by stirring in the rest of the cream and yogurt – and maybe even a little milk if needed.

3 Put everything for the syrup (except the zest) into a small saucepan and bring to the boil. Boil to reduce to a syrup (remember: it will get thicker as it cools). Strain to remove the cardamom, then add the zest and cook for another minute. Leave to cool. Serve with the rice pudding.

serves 6-8

200g (7oz) dried apricots, roughly chopped

100g (3½oz) sultanas

225ml (8fl oz) Moscatel (a Spanish dessert wine)

300ml (10fl oz) full-fat milk

300ml (10fl oz) double cream

a pinch of salt

½ tsp vanilla extract

3 large eggs, plus 1 large egg yolk

100g (3½oz) caster sugar

about 250g (9oz) bread (soft white rolls or brioche are particularly good) sliced

40g (1½oz) butter

icing sugar, to dust

bread-and-butter pudding is one of the great glories of British cookery, and it requires no skill and very little effort to make. I turn out lots of different versions, so once you have the basic recipe in your head, play around with it. You can use any sweet dessert wine instead of Moscatel in this apricot version, or sherry, Madeira or Marsala.

. . . . . .

apricot and moscatel bread-and-butter pudding

1 Put the apricots, sultanas and Moscatel in a saucepan. Bring to the boil, then turn off the heat at once, and leave to soak for anything from a couple of hours to overnight.

2 Bring the milk, cream and salt to the boil in a heavy-bottomed pan. Add the vanilla. Beat the eggs, extra yolk and sugar together. Stir in the warm milk and cream.

3 Butter the bread and layer it, buttered-side up, in an ovenproof dish, sprinkling on the fruit and alcohol as you go. Strain over the egg-an-cream mixture and leave to soak for 30 minutes to make the pudding lighter. Make sure there's no fruit sticking out of the custard to burn.

4 Put the dish in a roasting tin and add enough boiling water to come halfway up the sides of the dish. Bake in an oven preheated to 180°C/350°F/gas mark 4 for 40-45 minutes, or until puffy and set with a golden top. Leave to cool slightly, dust with icing sugar and serve with crème fraîche, or cream mixed with Greek yogurt.

and also...

...chocolate and pear bread-and-butter pudding
Make the pudding as above, but layer the bread with 3 sliced, cooked pears (poached in 250ml/9fl oz water, 75g/2¾oz caster sugar and the juice of 1 lemon) and 100g (3½oz) plain chocolate, cut into chunks.

...marmalade and whisky bread-and-butter pudding
Make as in the first recipe, but instead of the apricots and Moscatel, soak 300g (10½oz) raisins in 225ml (8fl oz) whisky. Layer the bread with the soaked fruit and 10 tbsp marmalade spread on the buttered bread.

...lemon curd and blueberry bread-and-butter pudding
Make as in the first recipe, but layer the bread with 10 tbsp lemon curd, spread on the buttered bread as you go, and 150g (5½oz) blueberries.

If you don't have an ice-cream machine, making your own can be a bit of a slog (all that hand stirring during freezing), but there are some spectacular ice creams on the market just waiting to be personalized.

• • • • • •

what to do with a tub of good ice cream

things to top ice cream

passion-fruit and orange sauce

Scoop the pulp and seeds out of 4 passion-fruit and press through a sieve. Put 175ml (6fl oz) orange juice in a saucepan and add the passion-fruit juice plus 2-3 tbsp of the sieved seeds along with 55g (2oz) caster sugar. Bring gently to the boil, then simmer over a medium heat for 12 minutes until slightly syrupy. Take off the heat and leave the sauce to cool – as it cools, it will thicken.

apricot and elderflower sauce

Cover 250g (9oz) dried apricots (the ready-to-eat type) with 600ml (20fl oz) water. Add the juice of 2 lemons and simmer very gently over a low heat for 30 minutes until the fruit has plumped up and is soft. Leave to cool, then purée with 5 tbsp elderflower cordial. Elderflower cordials come in different strengths depending on the brand, so taste to judge whether you want to add more or not.

hot fudge sauce

Put 175ml (6fl oz) double cream, 100ml (3½fl oz) golden syrup, 175g (6oz) soft brown sugar and a pinch of salt into a saucepan and stir over a low heat until the sugar dissolves, then add 25g (1oz) chopped chocolate. Cook over a low heat for about 15 minutes, stirring often, until it thickens. Add 30g (1¼oz) butter and stir to melt. Brilliant with sautéed apple slices and vanilla or nut ice cream.

marmalade sauce

Put 175g (6oz) marmalade into a small saucepan with 4 tbsp golden syrup, 50ml (2fl oz) orange juice and the juice of 1 lemon. Bring gently to the boil, pressing the marmalade with a wooden spoon to break it down, and serve hot or warm. Divine with a mixture of vanilla and chocolate ice creams.

ginger, lime and lemon grass syrup

Put 150ml (5fl oz) water, 125g (4½oz) caster sugar, a sugar-cube-sized knob of fresh root ginger, peeled and chopped, the juice of 2 limes (save the zest) and 2 lemon-grass stalks, bruised and chopped, into a saucepan and bring to the boil, stirring to help the sugar dissolve. Boil for 7 minutes then leave the syrup to cool and infuse for a good 40 minutes. Strain, add the lime zest and keep in the refrigerator. Good with vanilla or coconut ice cream, especially along with slices of fresh cold melon, pineapple or mango.

christmas sauce

Put 200g (7oz) good-quality mincemeat into a saucepan and add 75g (2¾oz) fresh cranberries and 25ml (1fl oz) orange or apple juice. Heat gently, then simmer for 10 minutes until the cranberries are soft but haven't burst. Add a slug of port or brandy and serve warm. Good with plain vanilla or a nut ice cream.

hot chocolate sauce

Melt 125g (4½oz) plain chocolate in a bowl set over a pan of simmering water. Add 100ml (3½fl oz) golden syrup and stir until melted. Add 2 tbsp any spirit or liqueur (rum, brandy, crème de framboise or Cointreau). Good with vanilla or coffee ice cream.

burnt sugar sauce
Put 350g (12oz) caster sugar into a saucepan with 250ml (9fl oz) water and 4 tbsp lemon juice. Bring to the boil, stirring to help the sugar dissolve, then let it boil to form a rich brown caramel. Take the pan off the heat and quickly add 250ml (9fl oz) double cream (stand well back as the caramel will spit). Stir and serve warm. Good with vanilla ice cream.

hot boozy cherries
Melt 25g (1oz) unsalted butter in a frying pan and throw in about 450g (1lb) stoned cherries. Add 100g (3½oz) caster sugar and the juice of ½ lemon. Keep sautéing the cherries and moving them around until they are tender and you have a thickish syrup around the cherries. Add a good slug of kirsch or grappa and spoon over ice cream. Great with chocolate sauce.

raspberry crush
Purée 200g (7oz) raspberries in a food processor with 30g (1¼oz) icing sugar. Sieve to remove the seeds. Roughly mash 100g (3½oz) raspberries with a fork and add to the sauce. Taste to see whether you want more sugar. Good with vanilla ice cream.

things to stir into vanilla ice cream

- Chocolate-coated coffee beans
- A bashed-up Crunchie bar
- A third of a jar of soft set preserves
- A few heaped spoonfuls of Christmas mincemeat
- Bashed chocolate-chip cookies
- Finely chopped preserved ginger and ginger syrup
- Smashed meringues – even better with raspberries
- A bag of bashed Maltesers
- Chopped-up *panforte* or nougat

things to do with vanilla ice cream

toasted brioche ice-cream sandwich
Toast slices of brioche and while still hot, halve them and sandwich with grated plain or milk chocolate and softened vanilla ice cream. Dust icing sugar over the top and serve wrapped in greaseproof paper.

fried *panettone* with melting ice cream
Fry slices of *panettone* in butter, sift icing sugar over the top and serve hot with warm sautéed apples or poached plums in winter, and sliced peaches or raspberries in summer, and good vanilla ice cream.

ice-cream stuffed baby brioche
Eaten in Sicily for breakfast but good after a lazy supper. Warm baby brioches in a low oven then stuff with vanilla ice cream and raspberries. Top with toasted flaked almonds and a sifting of icing sugar.

ice-cream cookie layers
Sandwich your favourite ice creams with your favourite biscuits. Put coffee, nut or orange ice cream, for example, into chocolate Hobnobs.

berry vanilla cones
Buy cones and fill with vanilla ice cream, fresh raspberries and the raspberry crush above.

a roll-call of sundaes
- Poached pear, toasted hazelnuts, vanilla ice cream and chocolate sauce
- Broken-up brownies, vanilla ice cream, raspberries and raspberry sauce
- Fresh pineapple, coconut ice cream, a slug of Malibu and ginger, lime and lemon-grass syrup
- And there are always more...

Most of us eat carbs and starches at least once a day, so it's good to know how to make them properly; myths abound, especially about rice and couscous. Potatoes are covered in the vegetable chapters, so here's how to deal with the other starches we most commonly cook.

· · · · · ·

an important bit about basics

couscous

A fabulous ingredient for the cook in a hurry. You can prepare couscous very quickly, and it can be as simple or elaborate as you like. All you need to do is put the couscous into a flat, shallow bowl and pour boiling water or stock over it. Allow two parts water to one part couscous. Stir in a couple of tbsp olive oil and season well. Cover the bowl with cling film. Once the liquid has been absorbed (it takes about 10-15 minutes), fork the grains to fluff them up and serve. You can do this in advance and leave the couscous to heat later, either by steaming, putting in a low oven (cover the dish with foil and heat at 180ºC/350ºF/ gas mark 4 for 20 minutes) or microwaving it. Fork the couscous again to fluff it up after heating. You can also serve couscous at room temperature.

If you prefer a buttery finish to an oily one, then stir in melted butter once the water or stock has been absorbed. Only do this with couscous you want to serve hot, though, or the butter congeals.

Add fresh lemon juice or rind, shredded preserved lemon, and handfuls of chopped soft herbs (parsley, coriander and mint are all great). Embellish as much as you like, adding plumped-up dried fruit (sour cherries, cranberries, chopped apricots, figs and raisins), sautéed onions (perhaps spiced with cumin, cinnamon or chilli), chopped fresh chillies, nuts (usually pine nuts, slivered almonds or pistachios) and fresh fruits such as pomegranate seeds or chopped fresh apricots or tomatoes.

bulgar wheat

Couldn't be easier or quicker, and bulgar has a gorgeous nutty taste. I now eat this more often than rice. Use two parts liquid to one part bulgar (you can use stock or water) and simmer gently, covered, for 10–15 minutes, until the liquid has been completely absorbed and the bulgar is fluffy. Leave the pan to sit, covered and off the heat, for 5 more minutes. Season and fork through.

As with rice, you can sauté some onion in butter or oil before adding the raw bulgar and liquid to the same pan. If you want to add other ingredients to make a pilaff, cook them separately and add once the bulgar is cooked. Olive oil, melted butter, herbs and lemon juice are all good for improving the flavour. Beyond that, embellish it just as you would couscous or rice.

rice

I'm dealing here with long-grain rice, the type most often cooked as a side dish. White long-grain is subtle and fragrant; brown is nuttier and nutritionally better for you. Choose whichever seems right for the dish it is accompanying and allow about 85g (3oz) per person.

To cook long-grain white rice, put the rice in a heavy-bottomed pan and add enough water to cover by

2.5cm (1in). Add salt, cover the pan and bring to the boil. Cook vigorously for 4–5 minutes, turning the heat down if there is a build-up of steam in the pan.

Take the pan off the heat. If you take a peek under the lid (be quick so that the steam doesn't escape), you'll see that the rice looks 'pitted', with lots of little holes in it. Leave the pan covered and allow it to sit for 10 minutes. The rice will cook in its own steam and absorb all the moisture. Check the rice to see whether it is cooked. If the liquid hasn't been completely absorbed, put the pan back on the heat for 2 minutes, then leave it to rest again for 5 minutes. If the liquid has been absorbed but the rice is still too firm, add a little water, put back on the heat for 2 minutes, then leave to stand for 5 minutes.

For long-grain brown rice, cook in a similar way to white rice but cover it with 5cm (2in) water, cook vigorously for 8 minutes, then turn the heat down very low, leave covered and cook for another 20 minutes on the heat, or until the water has been absorbed and the rice is soft and chewy.

You can cook both white and brown long-grain rice with stock instead of water, or sauté some chopped onion in the pan before adding the rice and stock.

It's okay to leave the cooked rice, covered, in a warm pan for 10-15 minutes before serving. Be sure to fluff the rice up with a fork before taking it to the table, and drizzle in some melted butter if you want to.

You can add all sorts of herbs, onions cooked with spices, cooked vegetables and dried fruits to dress the rice, and bits of warm cooked meat or fish to make a pilaff to serve as a main course.

pasta

Cook dried pasta in lots of boiling salted water. Salting the water improves the flavour, and an abundance of water gives the pasta room to move without the different shapes (or strands) sticking together. You don't need to add oil to the water, but you need to stir it once the water returns to the boil after the pasta has been added. This helps to separate the strands and lift pasta shapes from the bottom of the pan.

Allow 55g-115g (2-4oz) dried pasta per person. That sounds imprecise, but if you're serving pasta with a rich sauce (a creamy one, for example) you will serve a smaller portion than if you are dressing pasta with, say, a tomato sauce.

Drain pasta once it is *al dente*: this is just slightly firm to the bite. Overcooked pasta has a soggy texture and doesn't absorb sauce very well. You don't have to drain pasta too thoroughly, and you certainly don't need to pour water – either hot or cold – over it. Just put it into a heated bowl or back in the saucepan in which it was cooked and dress it immediately with the sauce. If you're in a flap and your sauce isn't ready yet, then douse the cooked pasta in olive oil or melted butter to stop it sticking together and get the sauce together quickly.

Dried pasta is not inferior to fresh pasta; it is just different, and it is what most Italians eat every day. Much of the fresh pasta sold here has a pappy texture (though Italian delis often sell good stuff), so you're better off with the dried type anyway. With dried pasta, the more expensive Italian brands are usually of superior quality.

an important bit about basics

index

sources

acknowledgments

The main constituents of all the recipes in the book can be picked up in local shops or supermarkets. I try to shop in small local shops as much as I can – it's good to get to know who you're buying from, and I don't want yet another estate agent or a Starbucks round the corner – but I realize that this isn't practical for everyone. I do depend quite a lot on my local Waitrose, and Ocado has been life-changing.

However, a well-stocked cupboard (good cans of anchovies, preserved lemons, spices, *et al*) does help you to make interesting food, so here are a few sources where you can find the more *recherché* ingredients, plus suppliers who stock easy-to-find ingredients, such as olive oil, but who are particularly excellent. Believe me, you can get quite addicted to opening parcels of lovely and exotic foodstuffs.

www.seasonedpioneers.co.uk for every spice you can think of.
www.coolchile.co.uk for dried chillies and hot sauces.
www.olivesetal.co.uk for olives and olive oil.
www.chocolate.co.uk for the obvious. It's the site for the Chocolate Society.
www.finecheese.co.uk for cheeses you didn't even know existed.
www.hebrideansmokehouse.com is my favourite smokery.
www.savoria.co.uk for all things Italian.

For fantastic food in all categories, from small farmers and artisan producers both here and abroad, try the following:

www.natoora.co.uk
www.chandosdeli.com
www.foodfullstop.com
www.provenancefinefoods.co.uk
www.delinostrum.com is based in Spain but supplies the UK. Brilliant – obviously – for all Spanish ingredients.
www.greatfood.ie is based in Ireland but will also send to the UK and has a great range of very high-quality stuff.

To search for difficult-to-find foods, log on to www.thegoodwebguide.co.uk to check out the list of specialist food suppliers which they collate and rate.

Many supermarkets now stock preserved lemons (a company called Belazu produces them), flower waters and more unusual types of rice, such as bomba, used for Spanish rice dishes. Smoked paprika (or *Pimentón de la Vera*) can be found in Waitrose and in Sainsbury's Special Selection. Pomegranate molasses is sold in Middle Eastern shops but if you don't have one nearby, Sainsbury's also sell this in its Special Selection.

This book has been created by an incomparable team. Commissioning editor Becca Spry, photographer Jonathan Lovekin, designer Miranda Harvey, editor Susan Fleming and home economist Sarah Lewis have been a joy to work with, putting more time and effort into the project than their jobs – strictly speaking – require. I would particularly like to thank Jonathan, Miranda and Sarah for making the shoot days so much fun. More often than not, it was like being on holiday. Jonathan just 'got' a feel for what we were trying to achieve and then surpassed what we had in mind. We can't divine why his pictures are so brilliant because he just seems to turn up, chat, take a few snaps and then enjoy lunch. But we're thrilled that they are. Sarah was always half a dozen steps ahead of me and is the most patient, kind, intuitive and visual collaborator a cook could hope for in the kitchen. I can't thank them enough.

Thanks, too, to my sister, Lesley, my parents, Robin and Joan, and my friend Eleanor Logan for tasting and testing and generally hanging out in my kitchen. Eleanor surpassed what a friend can reasonably be expected to do by eating more cakes and puddings than is good for a girl. My lovely friend Jenny Abbott has been telling me for years that this book is the thing that would most improve her life (actually she's already had most of the recipes over the phone or scribbled on bits of paper), so I'm glad she kept banging on about it. And I hope it will live up to her expectations...

No work would get done without my lovely nannies, Mari Smit and Milante Lombard, who look after me as much as they do the children and manage to be friends/PAs/sisters and extra mummies all at the same time. My friends Aliza O'Keeffe (who thinks she can't cook but can) and Johanna Oldroyd (a great baker and my personal expert in all things Scandinavian) generously gave recipes for dishes they have cooked and I have loved.

Lastly thanks to my gorgeous boys, Ted and Gillies, who put up with their mum being stuck at the computer or the cooker rather a lot of the time. Ted is only eight years old but took the beautiful photograph on page 38 (thank you for letting him, Jonathan), so he is obviously a food-lover. Actually, this book would never have happened if Ted's arrival hadn't had such an impact on my life and my cooking. The fact that Gillies then came along and can enjoy that cooking is the – very considerable – icing on the cake.

Please note that all eggs are large unless otherwise stated.